Tui De Roy Moore

GALAPAGOS

Islands Lost in Time

With an Introduction
by Peter Matthiessen

A Studio Book

The Viking Press · New York

To Jacqueline and André, my parents,
who taught me how to see,
and to Gil, my brother,
and Alan, my husband,
who shared with me the never-ending joy of discovery
and exploration in a land whose story pertains not to
mankind alone but to the entire world of living organisms

First published in 1980 by The Viking Press
625 Madison Avenue, New York, N.Y. 10022

Published simultaneously in Canada by
Penguin Books Canada Limited

Library of Congress Cataloging in Publication Data
Moore, Tui De Roy.
Galápagos, islands lost in time.
(A Studio book)
Bibliography: p.
1. Natural history—Galápagos Islands. 2. Galápagos Islands—
Description and travel. I. Title.
QH198.G3M66 574.9866′5 80-14058
ISBN 0-670-33361-1

Color printed in Japan by
Dai Nippon Printing Company, Tokyo
Printed in the United States of America
by The Murray Printing Company,
Westford, Massachusetts

Set in Century Schoolbook

Contents

Introduction

In late October of 1973, I accompanied Les Line, the editor of *Audubon* magazine, on an assignment in the Galápagos Islands; my article was to be illustrated by the editor himself, who happens to be a very fine photographer. Of all the curious creatures in the islands, the species whose portrait seemed most crucial was the giant tortoise, the last intact population of which occurred on the volcano of Alcedo, on the island of Isabela, which was sighted after several days of cruising by charter schooner through "the Encantadas." But Alcedo's rim, where the first tortoises might be encountered, was 3700 feet above sea level, and at dawn next morning, for one reason or another, Les did not feel up to the ascent. Pressing his camera into my hands, he hinted darkly that no Galápagos article could show its face in *Audubon* unaccompanied by the best photographs of *Testudo* ever taken. And so, weighed down by responsibility, I trudged away up the desert mountain and in the last one thousand feet followed an old tortoise path through heavy bracken to the summit.

> Walking north along the rim, I come upon a tortoise. It has a view of Darwin Crater, but tortoise and volcano are mutually oblivious; to be tortoise or volcano is enough. After a time of utter stillness, as if dumbfounded by the sight of my brown legs, the tortoise gets on with its slow chewing. . . .
>
> An august male emerges from a bush ten feet away to have a look at me. The large males mount the much smaller females wherever they can catch them—the females seek to avoid these crude encounters—and the mating is facilitated by a concave area on the male's plastron that permits a closer fit. In copulation, the triumphant male emits strange, primordial bellows, while the female maintains her customary silence. (A frustrated male may attempt to mate with boulders, though whether he bellows at these times is not recorded.) . . .
>
> A quarter-mile walk along the rim produces three more tortoises. Though all cease their slow browsing to gaze at me, none are flustered but the one that I pat companionably upon the carapace. It hisses wearily and shuts its hinge in languorous alarm, opening promptly as I depart and stretching out its neck to peer after man in slow, dim titillation.*

This was all very well,but although I met with a number of tortoises, I got not a single picture. The camera simply refused to function, although the inconsolable Les Line later suggested that the malfunction was directly attributable to human error. As the schooner weighed anchor, Les retired to his cabin, feeling seasick out of sheer depression.

At fortnight's end, arrived at the main anchorage at Santa Cruz, I confessed our plight to the schooner's captain, Richard Foster, who promptly suggested that I look at some photographs taken by a young girl there on the island. I shook my head: Line was a stickler for technical excellence, for which his magazine is justly famous; there was no place in *Audubon* for amateur snapshots. No, Richard said, she's really very good. And he sent word to the De Roys, a Belgian family, that someone wished to have a look at Tui's pictures. That afternoon, a sunburned, fair-haired girl turned up in a skiff at the ship's side, modest and shy and chaperoned by her mother, and I managed to persuade my doubting editor to attend a showing in the captain's cabin.

From the very first slide, we were stunned with pleasure and surprise, and even an unearned feeling of discovery; at nineteen, this pretty girl had already gone well beyond mere technical excellence. One after another, her pictures caught the gaunt brooding and spare light of these ocean volcanoes, at the same time transcending their subject to arrive at a quality more mysterious and universal.

I turned to look at the editor's face; it was a study in respectful disbelief. A few months later, to Les Line's great credit, one of Tui De Roy's beautiful studies of the giant tortoise was *Audubon*'s cover illustration, and a portfolio of "the best photographs of *Testudo* ever taken" accompanied the Galápagos article on the inside pages. Since then, her remarkable talent has matured, and meanwhile she has continued her exploration of the islands, which she knows as well as anyone alive; as her excellent text demonstrates, she is a well-informed, close, affectionate observer of the natural world. I know of no one better qualified to do a book on the Galápagos than Tui De Roy Moore.

—Peter Matthiessen

* From field notes published in *Audubon* magazine, September 1973.

Author's Note

The Galápagos Islands may be considered mere specks of land in a vast expanse of seas, the Pacific Ocean. On many world maps they do not even appear beside the enormity of the South American continent. Yet these islands are a unique entity, related to no other part of this planet. They contain mountains, forests, beaches, and bays unlike any others on the earth. Here animals and plants have evolved into unique forms; some have survived, scarcely changed, from prehistoric times.

For a long period the Galápagos were ignored by the human world. It is only recently that a few thousand people have begun calling these islands home, and I consider myself immeasurably fortunate to be one of them.

I would not trade my life experiences for anyone's. The atmosphere we children grew up in was often devoid of preestablished notions. We did not have many set rules, nor did we attend a school system with its fixed schedules and collective order. We communicated in several different languages and followed our interests and instincts freely. Nor were we herded into age groups, for there were not enough children to form them. We mingled with adults and related to them easily. Even though we had few neighbors, there were always special people, scientists and others, who visited the islands and enriched our lives, and whom we would not have had the opportunity to talk to elsewhere.

In this book I try to describe the natural world of the Galápagos Islands, my interest in nature being the one that has always governed my life. However, this is not intended to be a natural history, but an attempt at conveying the feelings that accompanied the discovery of a world of wild animals and plants, seashores and volcanoes; a personal voyage through life and through these largely unexplored islands.

In this work I would like to share my own discovery, the million ways in which these islands, so special and so mysterious, have brought me close to the living beings with whom we all share the earth. And with this collection of photographs I wish to impart to others the sheer wild beauty of the Galápagos.

Acknowledgments

A large number of people have been involved in the creation of this book. Over a span of ten or twelve years, since I was quite young, they have contributed in many ways, intentionally or unknowingly, to the assembling of this work. Some I may have forgotten, although their influence survives in my work.

I had to be convinced that I should write this book, and even more important, that I was capable of writing it. The turning point came when I was encouraged to write my first articles for nature magazines. Sometimes helped by luck and chance, but more often by those who invited me on interesting trips to special parts of these islands, I acquired a thorough collection of photographs of their natural history.

Throughout my childhood my parents stimulated me to investigate and attempt to understand everything around me, and it is to them that I owe my love for exploration and the patience that made the visual part of this book possible.

From my long-time friend David Cavagnaro I acquired the capacity for unbiased observation that is so necessary to feel at one with all living things. To him I am also indebted for the inspiration of his own books and a writing style that has permitted me to express my feelings freely. Ann Guilfoyle, though living in a modern world so very different from mine, never ceased to encourage me, giving me editorial advice and the support I needed.

My thanks go to Gail Davis for revising sections on biology, and to Patricio Ramón, Pete Hall, and Tom Simkin for their precious advice on the geology of Galápagos. To these people, and many others I have not mentioned, I will always be grateful for having profoundly enriched my life in the Galápagos. No matter where our different lives may take us, I know we will always share an attachment and deep love for these strange and special islands.

And last, I would like to express my profound appreciation to Miguel Cifuentes and my husband, Alan, for the years they have spent preserving and restoring the wild quality so essential to the very existence of these islands.

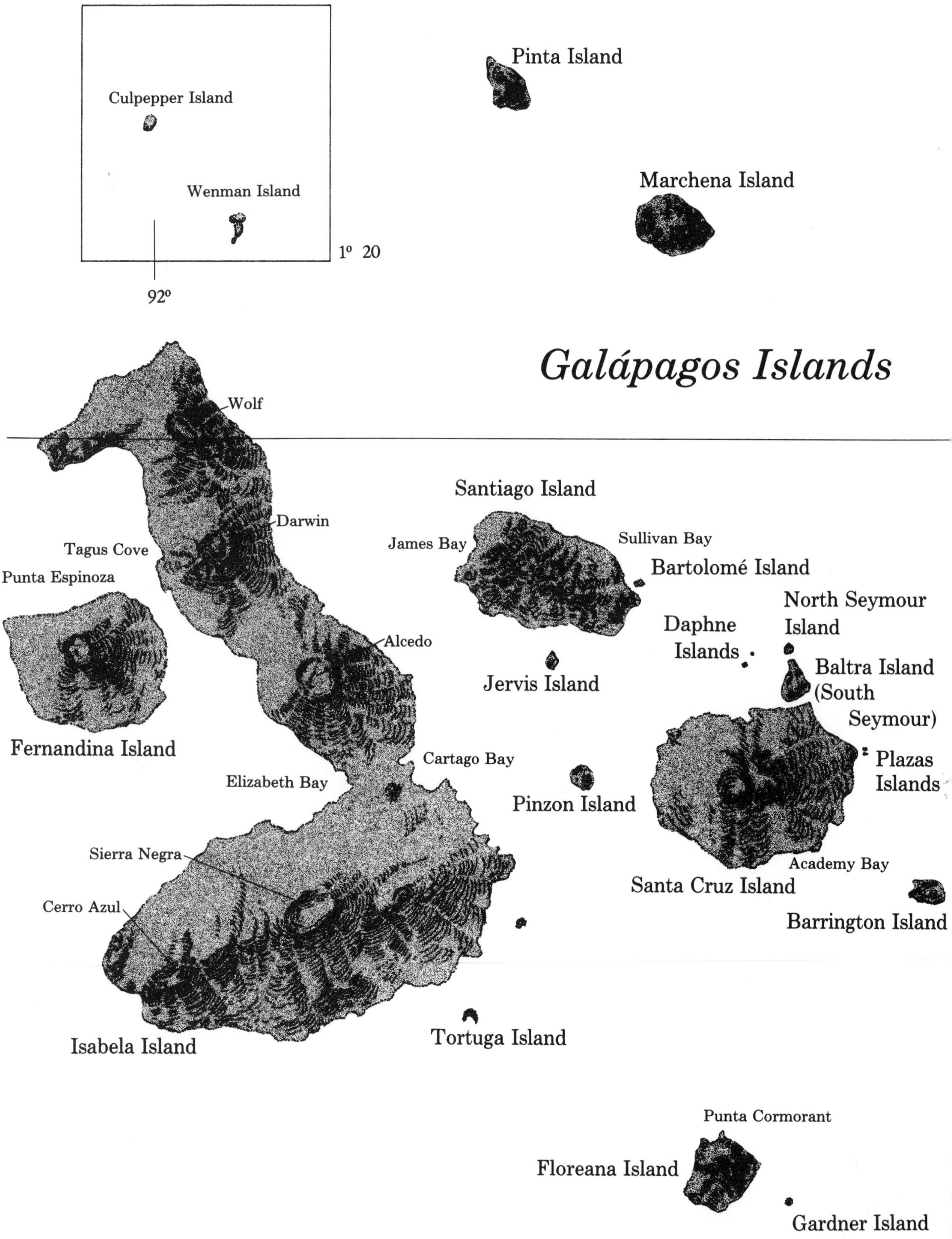
Culpepper Island
Wenman Island
1º 20
92º
Pinta Island
Marchena Island
Galápagos Islands
Wolf
Darwin
Tagus Cove
Punta Espinoza
Fernandina Island
Alcedo
Elizabeth Bay
Cartago Bay
Sierra Negra
Cerro Azul
Isabela Island
Tortuga Island
Santiago Island
James Bay
Sullivan Bay
Bartolomé Island
Jervis Island
Pinzon Island
Daphne Islands
North Seymour Island
Baltra Island (South Seymour)
Plazas Islands
Santa Cruz Island
Academy Bay
Barrington Island
Punta Cormorant
Floreana Island
Gardner Island

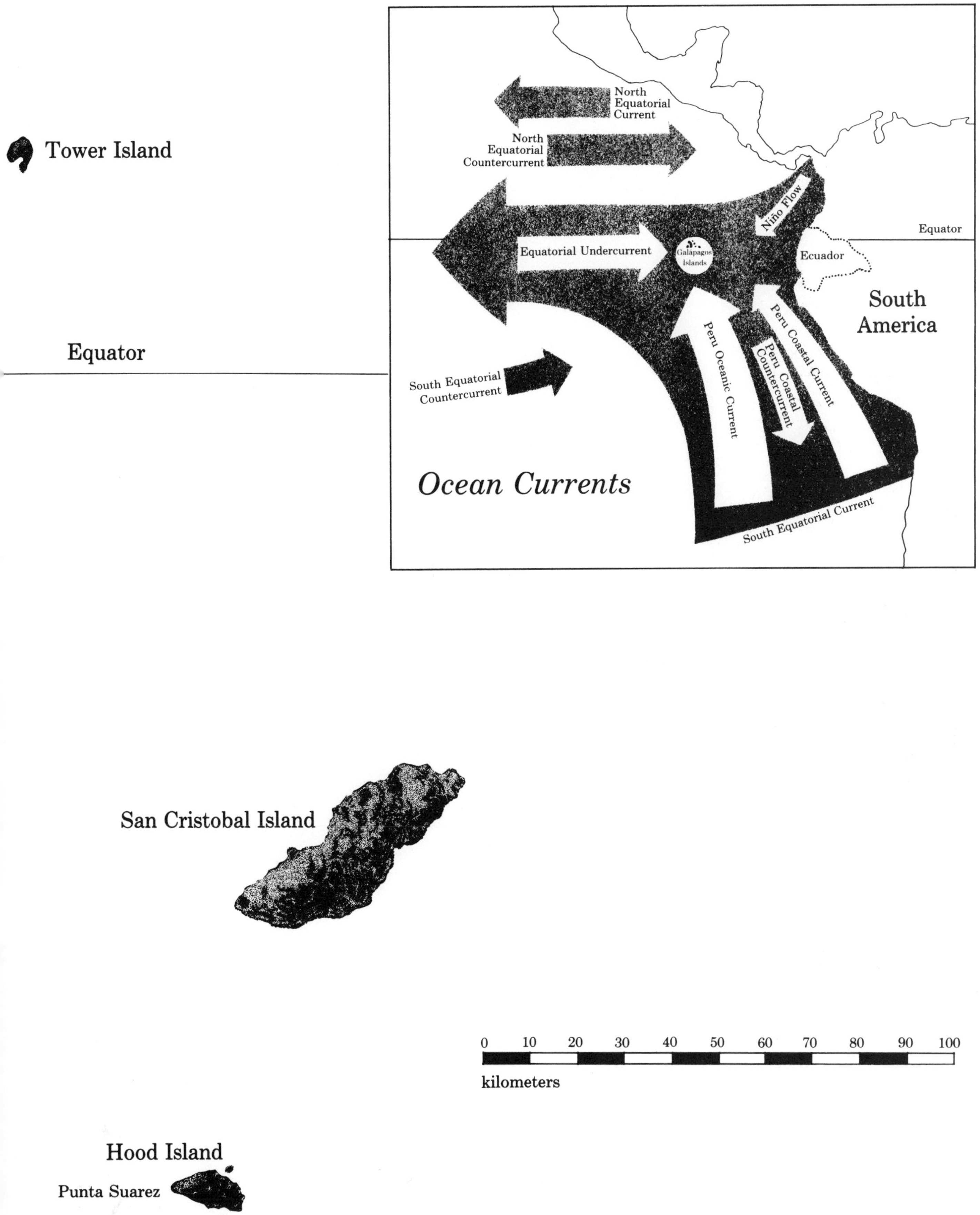

Ocean Currents
North Equatorial Current
North Equatorial Countercurrent
Niño Flow
Equator
Equatorial Undercurrent
Galapagos Islands
Ecuador
South America
Peru Oceanic Current
Peru Coastal Countercurrent
Peru Coastal Current
South Equatorial Countercurrent
South Equatorial Current
Tower Island
Equator
San Cristobal Island
Hood Island
Punta Suarez
0 10 20 30 40 50 60 70 80 90 100
kilometers

A Start in Life

Chapter One

Memories

There was a small white beach of extremely fine sand, deposited by millions of Pacific Ocean tides between two towering dark lava cliffs. The beach was smooth and shiny in the morning sun. The only marks on its surface were the large webbed prints where a pelican had landed, then walked to the water's edge. From the shade of an overhanging rock a small child ran, laughing, to splash in the lapping waves, and then back up to the dry powdery sand, still calling joyfully.

As these visions come to my mind now, that morning seems a very long time ago. It was in 1959; the five-year-old child was me. I lived with my parents in a lava rock house at the side of a bay on the island of Santa Cruz. Whenever we decided to visit the little white beach, great excitement always followed, for it held a wealth of secrets and grew to symbolize for me the wild nature of the Galápagos. One wave would uncover white polished shells, and the next would hide them again deep in the sand. There were quiet tide pools where small fish flitted from rock to rock and dark little crabs carefully probed the furry algae for food.

Some days my thoughts wander further back in time, to the year when I was two and we lived in the green highlands of the island. Views flash into my mind: the great elephant-ear plants twice as tall as I was; the thundering herds of wild cattle whose bellowing I tried to imitate with a little toy horn. At night flocks of nesting petrels swooped low over our camp. I never saw them, as they always came on moonless nights, but their eerie calls echoed in the mist. Straining memory, I try to recall the lengthy passage on the great freighter that carried us to this part of the world from the long, snowy winter that preceded our departure from Europe. But my memory blurs in the haze of time. A time that seems so infinite to my limited human mind, yet is so very short compared to the time it takes for a tree to grow, an island to form, or a Galápagos tortoise to live out its life.

When my parents were growing up, they loved all that was alive; they loved nature, and they loved the sea and the sun. But they lived in the city of Brussels, in Belgium, and there was war. When I was born near that city they were still young and they had a dream. They wanted to live their own life, to be independent and alone with the natural world close to the sea. So they went in search of that dream, and what they found were the Galápagos Islands. There is no paradise on earth, as dreamers often imagine, and my parents were wise enough to realize this. A dream is what one does with one's life, not what one finds. There was much adaptation and much toil ahead of them and they were ready for it. At first we lived in the moist interior of Santa Cruz Island, a three-hour walk from the coast. In the virgin forest my mother and father cleared a small plot of land to cultivate our food. Pigs and huge herds of cattle ate the crops and trampled the land. To protect us from these introduced farm animals that had gone wild, my father built a log platform raised off the ground, over which the tent my mother had sewn was placed on a thick mattress of bracken. The terrace was decorated with ferns and other epiphytes and around it grew many flowers raised from seed packets brought from Europe. Once every four to six months a small ship sailed from the port of Guayaquil in Ecuador, bringing out such essentials as flour, sugar, matches, and mail. Perhaps four hundred people lived on the island then, most of them Ecuadorians. A narrow winding path, which took half an hour to walk, led to our closest neighbors, a family of Norwegians. In my mind the trail seems endless, woven through tunnels of dense vegetation and overhanging vines and mosses where tiny birds searched for insect pupae. Along that trail was an old native guava tree. Its pale brown trunk was smooth, almost polished, like a windworn boulder by the sea, and at its base was an opening that led to its hollow interior. The shrill screams and squeals that frequently escaped from the dark gap both terrified and intrigued me. I was told that the hollow was a petrel's nest, but still I imagined many unknown beasts writhing in that obscure dwelling. One day my father decided to show me. He put his hand into the hole where the sounds came from and carefully brought to the light a large black and white bird. Flapping its great wings, it bit my father's finger and drew blood. Slowly he returned the bird to its nest, and I was astounded. Though my visions of grotesque beings had been shattered, I was happy I had seen one of the mysterious birds that called through the nights. But my fascination did not vanish, and still today I listen in wonder when petrel courtship calls echo through the cold, cloudy nights as the birds fly from the sea to their nesting grounds in the misty highlands.

We lived for one year under the luxuriant greenery of Santa Cruz. We grew flowers and harvested what few vegetables the feral pigs and cows left us. We saw the ferns grow, and watched thin vines span the narrow path in a day or two with their tendrils. And we knew where a pair of vermilion flycatchers had their nest in a soft clump of brown liverworts. We could feel the tropical seasons change, but at this elevation of two hundred meters rain and mist prevail much of the year, and my parents developed a longing for sunshine and a place by the sea. I was three when they decided to move to the coast, abandoning their little piece of land to be reclaimed by native tree ferns and shrubbery. By the seashore the weather was altogether different. Whereas the mountains had been shrouded in low, dense clouds, the areas by the sea were bathed in sunshine most of the time. The terrain was quite dry and the old lava surface was blanketed by a sparse forest of giant cacti and deciduous brush that grew leaves when the rains brought sufficient moisture. Here, among towering opuntia trees, my parents built a home out of lava blocks, near a small white beach and a saltwater lagoon.

Seasons on the Equator

On the equator it is not the shift in the sun's position that dictates the seasons; instead, the temperature of the sea and the ocean currents surrounding the Galápagos Islands determine the climatic patterns. During our southern winter from June to December cold currents flowing up from the southern parts of South America cool the waters around these islands, causing the cold season. Locally this is called the "garua" season, after the Spanish word for the mist and drizzle typical of that time. The cold water cools the air and loads it with humidity, whereas the atmosphere above this layer remains warm and tropical, preventing the sea-level air from rising and forming rain. It is only where this cold-air layer meets with the mass of the island at higher elevations that it precipitates into fog and fine rain. The coast remains totally dry throughout most of the season.

The weather may change radically during the other half of the year. From January to May warm waters move southward from the Gulf of Panama bringing torrential rains that may drench the arid coastal zone and the highland areas alike. However, these currents are erratic, and many years the warm season is almost as dry along the coast as the cold one is. The result of the garua season is the lush perennial forest in which we first lived, where small native orchids unfold their pale green flowers along the moss-covered branches of *Scalesia* trees. These trees are giant relatives of sunflower plants that have developed into arboreal form for lack of competitive types. They form large areas of damp quiet forest, their parasol canopies neatly touching at about ten or twelve meters above the ground. At about seven hundred meters, near the top of the island, the forest gives way to wind-swept grasslands. Here short-eared owls hunt, silently searching for rodents and small birds in the ground cover.

In the Green Highlands

Many times over the years I have returned to the highlands to wander among rolling green hills and shimmering bracken slopes on sunny days, and to explore rain-filled ponds and sphagnum bogs at the bottoms of small eroded craters of old extinct volcanic cones. Here and there the land is pitted with caves and crevices left by the great volcanic activity of long ago, and dips between the mountains shelter majestic tree ferns. Occasionally I can hear the call of a secretive little Galápagos rail beneath the grass and low foliage. The tiny birds have become nearly flightless in the isolation of their island home, where they live on the ground and rarely wander out in broad daylight. I sometimes lie motionless in a clump of dense bracken and, if I am lucky, the little black birds peer at me, intrigued, their small red eyes glinting like spots of fire in the dim light. Sometimes I find a tiny nest and speckled eggs in a grass bunch, or an entire small family scurrying through the weeds, mother and father first, followed by four or five minute black chicks. Here and there one of the adults will stop to catch a gray spider or an earthworm and feed it to one of the little ones.

The area where most of the rain falls, on the southern, wind-exposed slope of the island, is a vegetation belt consisting almost exclusively of one species of endemic small tree, the *Miconia.* This area, which forms a densely tangled microclimate, is especially fascinating to us as we explore its shady growth of epiphytic lichens and liverworts, and tender clumps of ferns of many kinds. In a narrow ravine filled with greenery I have observed the dark burrows of the nesting dark-rumped petrels remembered so vividly from my early years, and moss-filled ponds where dragonflies come to lay their eggs.

Childhood Learning

Our second, seaside home was in Academy Bay where a small fishing village already existed. The bay is divided into two halves separated by a long cliff running straight inland. On one side where the main part of the village was located, drinkable brackish water could be secured from crevices in the lava bed where fresh water drained from the mountains and mixed with seawater. On the other side no water could be found and only a few families lived scattered along the shore, most of them Europeans. This part of the bay was the most scenic, and even though living there meant that every drop of water had to be brought by rowboat from around the dividing cliff, this is where our house was built. When I was four and a half my brother was born, and since there was no doctor or hospital on the island, he was born, like all the other children, at home. Our childhood years were spent in carefree explorations by the edge of the sea, where we played games in the sand and made many little discoveries that brought us ever closer to nature. Near our home was a saltwater lagoon that became flooded with every full moon tide. Schools of little fish would become trapped, and herons, egrets, stilts, gulls, and sometimes pelicans would catch them. And there were the whimbrels, ruddy turnstones and sandpipers that we knew had traveled thousands of miles on their migrations from northern North America. They would eat the gray fiddler crabs with huge orange claws, which we had seen locked in combat in the muddy shallows. Nearby was a coarse white beach, and next to it were dense mangrove thickets where we would go climbing, thinking we were monkeys. We swung from branch to branch and between the long aerial roots. Sometimes we fell, but we never hurt ourselves for the tangles were so thick that we always became suspended in them. In the deep shady spots yellow-crowned night herons slept away the daylight. Occasionally a pair nested here and their shaggy young peeped quietly in a big nest of mangrove twigs. When the tide was low, we often searched for seashells. On the wide rocky reef we knew where the cone shells lived beneath the coral grit, in tide pools where sand-colored blennies nibbled at our feet. We also knew where we might find the shiny chocolate-brown cowry shells with white spots. If we secured one, we would present it to an octopus whose home we knew. He would grab it greedily with his long tentacles covered with suction cups. The next day we could retrieve the cowry at the edge of his entrance hole, clean and perfect, with only a minute acid-drilled hole in the shell that had enabled the octopus to extract and eat the soft animal within. Some octopuses were more reliable than others. A few would keep the shell for several days or discard it far away from their holes, whereas others would always have pushed the beautiful shell in front of their burrow by low tide on the following day.

In the warm season we spent endless hours every day swimming off the small beach, splashing and diving. When the weather became particularly hot and calm, myriads of microscopic sea organisms would glow at night. In a tranquil mangrove-surrounded cove this flashing blue phosphorescence would sometimes attain astounding degrees, the slightest movement in the water provoking showers of light. As we rowed our small skiff quietly on moonless nights, every darting fish, every small shark, would leave a sparkling trail, like so many shooting stars in a black watery sky; and green sea turtles would be outlined in a blue glow dozens of meters away.

We learned many things from our surroundings. But we also had to learn our responsibilities early in life. The sea with its waves and sharks could be dangerous to us, and so could the cliffs, crevices, and rugged rocky shores. We learned our limitations and how to judge what was safe and what might not be. As we grew older we got to know the back country where the lava terrain seemed to bare its back beneath the groping roots of the dry vegetation. It never ceased to amaze me how these plants drew nourishment from a place where no dirt or humus was visible among the rocks. On this rugged land giant cacti grew in abundance. There were two distinctive types, *Opuntia* and *Jasminocereus,* both majestic trees with smooth stately trunks. Their growth might take centuries, for no human observer has ever recorded the complete cycle. Here small finches in great numbers make their living. Some gray, some black, they flit along the ground and in low shrubbery and nest in the tall cactus trees. These are the famous Darwin's finches, and we learned to recognize the different species by the varying shapes and sizes of their beaks, which were well adapted to the sorts of seeds they feed on. They lived all around our house and frequently carried away pieces of thread and string to line their nests. They inspected our garden for extra tidbits and some individuals learned to collect crumbs from our table. Each bird had its own signal to attract our attention. One friendly female would sit on our heads pulling our hair, then fly to the door to indicate she wanted it opened, either to enter and feed or, if she was already inside, to leave again. Year after year she returned with her mate, who had the habit of scraping his bill along the metallic insect screen at the door to get his share of cookies. At the end of the warm season they would bring their chirping fledglings to the bonus food. One year they separated for no reason that we could have guessed, and each returned with a new mate. They became quite antagonistic, and remained so. One day she somehow entered our house while we were away and drowned in a jar of aquatic plants. We were very sad, and have missed her ever since. She had been our trusting friend for many years and she died because of our carelessness.

These finches have a very long life span, whereas temperate-region passerines, or perching birds, may live only a couple of years. As far back as I can remember the little birds were part of our life, singing their raucous two-syllable song by our windows and cracking huge seeds in the croton trees along our path. The finches exploited the seeds yielded by the dry scrub to perfection, while little lava lizards barely six inches long did the same with sparse insect life, hopping deftly from rock to rock, stalking flies, moths, ants, and spiders. The males were streaked in varying tones of gray and each owned a territory covering a few feet of land, which they defended fiercely against any intruders. Here one to three females, readily differentiated by their bright orange throats, could live with the male and in turn fend off all other females. They lived everywhere around us and some even claimed a section of our house as their territory. Those that were used to seeing us would often become very tame, running to snatch any fly we might kill and, when the day was cool, even sitting on our bare feet for warmth. We learned many details about their private lives and about the variability of their individual personalities, and that certain lizards and finches learned to make use of the new opportunities we offered them while others didn't.

We also learned many practical skills from our parents, how to fish and how to free-dive and catch big spiny lobsters for the table. My mother rarely bought meat in town; instead, my father would go out weekly to hunt the many introduced goats that had invaded the islands. When I became old enough he took me along and I learned to shoot and butcher the goats myself. On returning home, I would dry the beautiful skins, which were shiny black or reddish brown in color. It always seemed a great shame to kill these splendid animals, but it was a matter of survival. We were the predators and we depended on other living things for our own life. We never killed any of them unless we could make use of the meat for food.

Shortly after my brother was born my father built a small boat and for some time he made a living as a fisherman the way most of the inhabitants of Academy Bay did. From October to March they fished for grouper on a hand line and cut it open to salt and dry it in the sun. The fish were then shipped in bulk to the mainland port of Guayaquil to be sold as a traditional Easter food. Every morning we would pull a long net along the beach to catch bait, and seabirds would always flock around us to try and snatch one of the unfortunate small fish we captured. One day a young lava heron that had just left its nest approached hesitantly. I remember patiently dangling a minnow from my fingers and slowly gaining the bird's confidence until he became quite tame and trusting. As he grew older, his mature plumage revealed that "he" was a female. I named her Savins, although I have no idea how that name originated in my mind, and whenever I called her, she would come flying out of the mangroves to meet me. Frigate birds and pelicans always came to get their share when the grouper was being cleaned. The frigates would soar quietly in the afternoon sky, waiting for a tidbit to be tossed overboard. When this happened they would all drop suddenly, like bundles of feathers vibrating through the air. For a moment they would flutter agitatedly over the water until the deftest one picked the piece of fish gut neatly off the surface. Pelicans would sit on the water all around the boat, beaks half open, their beady eyes shining expectantly. They nested nearby in the low mangroves and their hungry young could be heard hissing hoarsely whenever a parent bird approached the nest.

Around the house we had a small herd of tame goats. They were free and roamed the back country at night to feed, returning every morning to give us their milk. We tried to breed white or light-colored hornless ones so that the hunters would not mistake them for the wild ones, which were dark. The small young were kept at home during the afternoons and nights while their mothers wandered far inland. They were beautiful and vigorous, and we spent hours watching them spring about playfully, exploring every corner of the house, or running with them along the beach. But times changed. More and more people came to live on the island and some found that they could make good money exporting live wild goats to the mainland on the small freighter. They rounded up the goats with uncontrolled packs of dogs, some of which ran amok and killed many of our tame goats. Finally we decided that we would do our little herd justice by killing them ourselves rather than letting them be torn apart by the teeth of frenzied dogs. When our goats were gone, it seemed that part of our childhood had disappeared too.

Growing Up Free

There were about eight other children in the neighborhood when we were growing up. They had come from different nations and no one language ruled among us. Most of them spoke German, while a few knew only English, and my brother and I used French between us. As a result we quickly learned the different languages and used them interchangeably when the need arose. All the children were tutored at home in their own mother tongues. My parents felt that if we were to live in this part of the world, we should know how to read and write and be given some instruction in mathematics. Insofar as it was possible, our mother gave us a lesson every morning, although there were often other, more important things that occupied our days, so that the lesson would have to wait. Many of the neighborhood children later spent several years in Ecuador, Germany, or the United States to complete their education. This opportunity was also offered to me, but I finally decided against it, preferring to stay here and continue to learn on my own. Instead of entering the competitive world of college degrees and jobs, I began to explore more intensely around me, searching for a more profound understanding of the ways of living things and the mysteries of natural phenomena. By now my parents had acquired another boat, slightly larger than the first. It was twenty-three feet long and equipped with motor and sail, and in it we could explore parts of the archipelago away from our home island of Santa Cruz.

Little by little progress invaded the Galápagos. There were more people and more facilities. A road was built into the highlands and farmers brought agriculture farther inland. Very few haunting petrel calls still pierced the fog-laden garua night. Airplanes began flying in weekly from Ecuador, bringing increasing numbers of visitors who toured the islands on cruise ships. Yet we discovered as we traveled to the many uninhabited places that the Galápagos don't change so easily. Sailing the frothy sea bordering long stretches of barren lava coastlines, we can still go for days and days without noticing the slightest human trace.

The New Land Appeared

Chapter Two

In the Beginning

When my brother, Gil, and I were teenagers, we traveled to many of the Galápagos Islands, and numerous impressions of those trips remain profoundly engraved in our memories. I remember one day sitting on a flat rock slab at the shore of Fernandina Island. The jagged lava of this bare volcanic land was partially covered by low damp strands of fog along the water's edge. The warming morning sun quietly dispersed the thin watery vapors, revealing the rugged terrain beyond the cove and the ponderous shape of the mighty volcano high above. I knew this was probably one of the youngest islands in the group. The lone volcano was the result of relentless successions of thousands, or millions, of volcanic eruptions that had started on the ocean floor and now reached almost fifteen hundred meters above sea level. Looking off at the dark-streaked flank of the mountain, I thought of how this activity was still going on today and how it seemed never to have waned since it had started, and I tried to imagine how it had all begun. We know that the beginning was sometime during the very last moments of the earth's formation. Continents had already drifted very close to their present positions and many of the animals and plants of today already lived on them. Then the mysterious process of volcanism began for the first time in this part of the world, depositing a new structure beneath the sea. The volcanic activity occurred somewhere on the equator one thousand kilometers or so from the closest land. Something began to shudder on the eastern Pacific Ocean floor, and fear spread among the creatures of those depths. Thick layers of bottom sediments and basaltic rocks bulged and intensive heat disturbed the cool oceanic depths. Eventually a bit of fresh, glowing lava started to spread. Or perhaps the beginning was much more gentle, hardly noticeable. Nonetheless it represented the birth of a new volcanic formation that would one day become the Galápagos Islands.

Slowly, ever so slowly in our human scale of time, the relentless process continued. Submarine volcanic eruptions succeeded one another when fissures opened, yielding to the pressures of the convulsive magma below. Where the crust was more flexible, the molten matter was withheld and the entire ground rose beneath the sea. Millennia went by as this tremendous work transformed the ocean floor.

Fissure systems became established and cones of eruptive matter began to accumulate at their weakest points. Through time they continued to build in volume, reaching always farther upward. Even at this early stage marine invertebrates of many kinds must have attached themselves to the flanks of the cones, increasing in number and variety as the tops of the volcanoes approached the surface of the ocean and the life-giving sunlight. Then one day, probably around four million years ago, one of these growing volcanic cones pierced the sea. For some time it continued to explode as cold water and hot molten lava bubbled together, sending dark streaks of ash and huge thundering steam clouds high into the atmosphere. As more matter was deposited, water was sealed out of the volcano, and the new island entered a phase of gentle activity. Subsequent lava flows were more solid and could resist the action of the surf. The island continued to expand. To the seabirds who might have seen it as they flew over the ocean, it had a stark, barren appearance, with heaped accumulations of ash and scoria, and black slabs of lava jutting toward the blazing sun.

A Geography of Change

As the first island grew above water, others pierced the ocean surface next to it. Some appeared soon, others did not show for thousands of years. The order in which the islands appeared is one of the many unanswered questions that may have great meaning in relation to the diversity of life now found on these islands. Undoubtedly, there was much activity after the first islands became established. Pressures beneath the ground shifted, topography changed, and parts of or perhaps even entire islands sank. Some grew larger and coalesced, so that several small islets were fused into one imposing mass. Certain islands never erupted at all but worked their way out of the seas as a result of the upheaval of submarine lava flows, which rose in great fractured blocks and rifts into the air. A few of these still stand today, and to our searching eyes their rocks appear to be the oldest in the group. But perhaps some of the original rocks on the active islands are hidden beneath dozens upon dozens of more youthful lava flows. This slow building process is still going on today. Almost every year new eruptions and lava flows streak the flanks of the already massive volcanic edifices, and many fumaroles, constantly emitting vapors and gasses, mark their enormous craters.

The Galápagos are near an area of intense undersea volcanic activity. Just to the north is the Galápagos Rift, a region of complicated topography dotted with countless submarine fumaroles. Extending a thousand kilometers to the east, this fractured zone joins the East Pacific Rise, a tremendous fissure in the earth's crust that feeds the spreading line between the tectonic plates of the Pacific Ocean floor. One of these sections of the earth's surface is the Nazca Plate, which, through continental drift, carries the Galápagos cluster slowly toward the coast of South America, where the continent overrides the oceanic plate. Thus the Nazca Plate is forced down to be reabsorbed into the earth's mantle. At the present rate of movement it will take about fourteen million years for the Galápagos Islands to be inexorably engulfed by the interior of the planet.

The volcanoes that form the Galápagos Islands are known as shield volcanoes. These are large, low, symmetrical cones made up of thousands and thousands of thin fluid basaltic lava flows. Some of the islands are a conglomeration of a larger number of small cones, which gives them a very irregular shape. Others consist of one or a few very large shield volcanoes rising many thousands of feet from their base beneath the sea to their present height above water. These volcanoes are dome shaped in outline and are marked at their center by an enormous caldera. The caldera is a gigantic crater created by the caving in of the summit of the mountain. The calderas in Galápagos volcanoes range in diameter from two to ten kilometers. The two westernmost islands in the archipelago, Isabela and Fernandina, between them comprise seven huge active volcanoes. To this day the slow growth of these islands continues, as new streams of lava are added from time to time to their already streaked flanks.

These volcanoes are one of the utterly fascinating spectacles in nature. When I let my glance wander across their starkly decorated slopes, I soon lose all sense of time and distance contemplating the intricate patterns of gray, brown, and black lava flows forever overlapping. The flanks lift ever more steeply near the summit, which from below looks smooth and rounded, silhouetted against the sky. It is only when one climbs to the top that one discovers the extraordinary pit of the caldera that scars this dome. The view drops, sometimes a thousand meters, into a world elaborated by the deep, mysterious energy of the planet's interior. Volcanic ash, clearly cut crevices, boulders, cliffs, and dark lava flows combine into a tormented landscape, punctuated here and there by the white plumes of steaming fumaroles.

Origins of Life

Even here, in one of the most active volcanic regions of the world, living creatures of many forms subsist and even thrive. Among the variegated patterns of lava flows on the flanks of Fernandina there are light-colored patches or "islands" of vegetation that have for a long time escaped the marring effect of repeated volcanic outbursts. Many delicate and magnificently adapted plants grow here and orange-colored land iguanas roam and small finches nest among them. On the great shields of the island of Isabela where vegetation has blanketed the land, giant tortoises live and reproduce slowly over the centuries. Even the barest web reveals the constant presence of life.

In the humid forest of *Scalesia* trees in the highlands of Santa Cruz Island a great variety of tender leaves reaches out for light, overlapping in infinite numbers, and I began to consider the endless chain of hazards and chances that might have brought them together here to vie for the vital sunlight. Between the dangling ferns and brown and yellow lichens tender patches of club mosses cover the trunks of the trees. I look more closely and see their perfect feathery stems stretching upward. The sun, filtering through the foliage, catches the golden stalked sporangia, making them glitter in many tones of amber. Could this have been the very first type of plant to colonize the new Galápagos land?

The formation of the archipelago must have been well under way when this very special event took place. Perhaps in a shaded fissure a few moss spores, so minute that they almost escaped terrestrial gravity, were deposited by a breeze. They had been carried a great distance on the wind, probably from somewhere in South America. In great numbers these spores and other small seeds had been dropped on the new land before this, and all had died on the bare, sunbaked lava. But this time the spores had by chance drifted into a crevice with just the right amount of moisture to allow them to begin their growth, and soon they were performing the miraculous process of photosynthesis for the first time on this remote land. Once established, they expanded successfully, spreading to the surrounding fissures, and with time other small plants germinated among them.

When tropical downpours drench the forests along the coast of South America many streams and rivers overflow, tearing away branches and trees and entire clumps of tangled vegetation. These are hurtled downriver by flash floods, which frequently carry them out to sea. Some large and buoyant clumps act like floating islands to support many different plants, seeds, and seedlings, as well as terrestrial invertebrates. Occasionally they even carry reptiles, mammals, or stunned, rain-soaked birds. Most of the clumps disintegrate and sink upon reaching the open ocean, leaving their unfortunate passengers to drown. But once in a very great while a clump is so intricately entangled that it remains afloat, drifting away from shore with the currents. Occasionally a hollow tree trunk protecting some small inhabitants in its core floats out to sea. Undoubtedly most of these precarious castaways never see land again and die after days, weeks, or months at sea. Only a small percentage of living organisms arrive safe and sound on the barren Galápagos shores.

Once on land, a considerable task awaits the living creature—that of finding without delay a reasonable substitute for the habitat it lost, or an environment it might adapt to for survival. If it is to become a successful inhabitant, it will later have to surmount another huge problem, locating a mate and an adequate environment in which to rear its young.

Considering all these difficulties, it seems a wonder that there are any plants or animals on such isolated islands. Yet many hundreds of different species succeeded in establishing themselves on the Galápagos over the millennia. Not all were transported by means of vegetation rafts. Some plant seeds and small insects became airborne and traveled hundreds of miles with the wind, like the spores of the small club moss. The large seeds of certain trees drifted with ocean currents for long periods before germinating in fresh water. And of course a number of animals arrived by their own means of propulsion, either swimming or flying.

There must have been a fantastic number of these arrivals, widely dispersed in time. Plants and animals again and again were washed onto the rugged shores, only to die soon thereafter, unable to survive the new and arid environment. In order for any of these to become fixed, a careful sequence had to develop. A few plants that do not depend on organic matter had to grow first, permitting others to use what they created, thus allowing a new fragile ecosystem to form.

While the little club-moss colony thrived, lichens also found places to accomplish their delicate symbiosis. (Or did these come before the moss?) Tiny pockets of humus were left by decomposing bacteria, more plants discovered nooks they could grow in, and small insects began filling new niches while feeding on these plants and bacteria. Seabirds that made their living in this part of the ocean visited the young islands frequently, and began using their shores to nest on occasionally. They brought with them other forms of life from other shores, for migrating birds can carry seeds, insects, or snails stuck to their feathers and feet for hundreds and even thousands of kilometers over open water without touching down. Some seabirds became permanent residents and flies and other insects made use of the organic debris around their nests.

This colonization took place over a tremendously long period, but speeded up as more types of living organisms began finding interdependent ways to settle and reproduce, and the new island community grew more important. With each addition, great adjustments had to be made and some of the established forms were wiped out by more successful ones. But still, at this early point, they were mostly mainland species that had come from Central or South America, castaways that could not continue to live in the way for which they were best fitted. They had to make use of another environment and other food resources, and for the most part they were poorly adapted. However, their numbers increased, and the competition caused a fantastic process to take place: natural selection.

Evolution

Many species could not readily fly, swim, or be carried by the wind or by birds, and so a small group of individuals were forced to reproduce in complete isolation on their new island home, cut off from their ancestral stock hundreds of kilometers away. The chances that another member of the same species would arrive before countless years elapsed were very slim indeed. Through this isolation the process we now call evolution ensued. The hereditary material in each type was not crossed and recrossed in a large genetic pool, but instead every individual passed on a large quantity of personal traits to a great number of descendants. Because the slightest improvement represented a significant advantage, the genes governing that improved characteristic were selected out and transmitted to further generations, whereas in a large, fluid population these new traits would more likely be genetically flooded out by the already stabilized pattern. Evolution is still only a theory, because our human life span is not long enough to enable us to witness its process in a natural environment. The results only become visible through the perspective of seemingly endless time. Most of us now accept that the phenomenon exists, and *evolution* is the word we use to describe the gradual change from one species into a new one or several others.

Islands such as the Galápagos have greatly increased our understanding of evolution because they are isolated from their mainland source of life and because each individual island is separated from its neighbors. Like a simplified display of a complicated formula, the islands demonstrate how isolation and evolution have worked together to form new and different types of animals and plants. Some types can be traced back to their distant origins, and many terrestrial animals exhibit variations from island to island, having clearly diverged from one common ancestry. A strange and gentle harmony exists among them, for they were able to evolve in the almost complete absence of predators, and many peculiar and unexpected forms ensued.

Darwin's Finches

Of all the Galápagos animals the ones that have played the most important role in unraveling the mechanisms of evolution are the thirteen species of Darwin's finches.

On the topmost stem of a giant cactus one of these little birds with an enormous blunt bill sings to the morning his low-keyed, repetitive two notes. Nearby, another, looking very similar in size and coloration, is actively prodding into the bright yellow blossom of an *Opuntia* cactus. His beak, however, is thick at the base, long, and pointed, and as he feeds deep within the flower, his head becomes covered with powdery pollen. In another setting somewhere along the shoreline still a different form, this one with a tiny obtuse beak, flits among an immobile colony of marine iguanas, here and there picking a few blood-filled ticks from the scaly black skin of the reptiles.

These three examples beautifully illustrate the great versatility in adaptation achieved by the Darwin's finches. There are many cases in the world where one species of animal has radiated and diverged into a number of different species, but what is so special about these little birds is that at the present stage of their evolutionary course they are still closely enough related to make this process very obvious. All species of Darwin's finches bear a striking resemblance to one another in shape and behavior, and all of them build round, domed nests with side entrances. Yet each species has developed in such a way as to exploit its own specific type of food.

When the original finch population arrived from an unknown mainland source, the environment in which they landed was extremely different from the habitat they had left. But they encountered a great asset: very few, if any, vertebrates lived on the islands to compete for the extensive food sources available there. In order to make better use of these riches the early finches began to diverge into new forms. Today we have the cactus finch, which uses its long pointed beak on the flowers and fruits of the cactus trees, and the tiny warbler finch, which resembles a true warbler in song and behavior. The large tree finch has a sharp, parrotlike beak, and the woodpecker finch, although physically poorly suited to its environment, has adapted to take the place of the absent woodpecker family. Inspecting deep branches for insect larvae and termites, it swings its small body to hammer at the bark and clambers acrobatically up and down vertical tree limbs. It lacks the long, probing tongue of the real woodpeckers, but it has developed a most remarkable substitute by making use of a carefully selected tool. Usually it chooses a sharp cactus spine, which it breaks to the desired length, and by holding the utensil as a direct extension of its beak, it can extract grubs from deep cracks in the wood. This is one of very few instances of the evolution of a tool-using habit in the world of birds.

Why Marine Iguanas?

One day on the rugged lava shore of Punta Espinosa on Fernandina Island I watched the sun sink low in the western sky and cast a strange glistening sheen on the dark undulating sea, which looked like the surface of a shining solidified mass. Near the water's edge groups of nearly black reptiles huddled. They had long scaly tails, short legs with sharp claws, and thin spiny crests running down their backs. They have been described as utterly hideous, yet in this natural setting they were starkly beautiful. These were the unique Galápagos marine iguanas. Even though I had seen them almost every day as I was growing up, I sat down now to ponder their presence. Great lazy waves came breaking in behind them like flashing white forms in the dimming light, and they moved closer together to keep warm during the approaching night. One of them turned his head and examined me for a few seconds, then settled into sleep. I have always wondered how these iguanas came to depend on the sea for their living, a feat accomplished by no other known lizards in the world. Perhaps their ancestors arrived clinging to a log, or a tangle of logs and branches, forest dwellers cast upon this desolate shore. But how did they adapt to the marine environment, ingesting and processing seawater, swimming and diving for a diet of algae? Vegetation must have been scanty at that time, for it is still sparse along most of the shores. Algae could have supplemented the iguana population's nutrition, enabling them to survive and multiply, adapt and evolve. But many episodes in the process are still a mystery.

The sun sank below the horizon on the ocean, and a fine mist from the waves drifted across the low land, picking up an orange reflection. Against this diffused light the iguanas I had been watching were silhouetted in every detail, resembling the jagged shapes of the barren lava around them. Another night was coming, and after it another day, in a dazzling sequence that allows all living things to change, to readjust their functions, to survive.

The Endless Discovery

Chapter Three

The Arrival of Man

For a very long time the Galápagos Islands remained an environment known only to those living forms that had so magnificently adapted to their special conditions. Chance had not brought many predators to colonize these shores; there were no carnivores and the animals did not have to depend on their instinct of fear for survival. This idyll suddenly ended in the year of 1535, on the 10th of March, when a Spanish bishop accidentally sighted the first island. He had been sailing from Panama to Peru when his ship was becalmed and for several days he had been carried helplessly westward by the currents, in the same fashion as the early animals and plants that floated here long before him. And so Fray Tomas de Berlanga discovered the Galápagos. But he and his companions may not have been the first men to set foot on these shores. An Inca legend tells of a king who long ago traveled on a distant voyage in the Pacific to some remote islands, one of which he called "Island of Fire." Were these the Galápagos? If so, the Inca monarch did not alter or harm the native wildlife, as so many later visitors have. Indeed, with the bishop's landfall a sad story began for the gentle inhabitants of this place. "Galápagos" was the Spanish name given to the giant tortoises living in great numbers there, referring to their saddlelike carapace. The islands gradually gained fame among early seafarers for these tortoises, and eventually inherited their name. Over the centuries many sailing ships of various trades and nations anchored along the forbidding shores and gathered thousands of these helpless reptiles. The sailors stowed them below decks where they served as a source of live meat that would survive for many months without food or water during long ocean voyages. Relentlessly and remorselessly, the crews of these boats searched farther and farther inland for this fresh source of protein, and the tortoises gradually grew fewer in number. It has been estimated that several hundred thousands were taken during the last three centuries. The tortoises had adapted into different races on different islands, and many of these were nearing extinction with every year that passed. At the same time many of man's domestic animals were inadvertently or intentionally disembarked, and these began to affect and sometimes shatter the fragile ecosystems. Dogs and pigs attacked the larger vertebrates, while cats, rats, and mice fell upon the smaller animals. In the meantime, cattle, horses, donkeys, and goats destroyed the native vegetation. It is the same sad tale that is told practically every place in the world that the plundering white man reached in his constant effort to explore and colonize. Man encountered nature violently wherever he went, for he had not yet realized that he was out of balance with it. But in the eyes of those great navigators of the seventeenth, eighteenth, and nineteenth centuries, this plundering was a matter of survival. Their voyages were long and perilous, and they perceived the Galápagos Islands as threatening, harsh, and depressing. Unless they became familiar with every detail of the rugged shores, they could easily perish of thirst, for fresh water was always scarce on this porous volcanic land. The eighteenth century especially saw many visitors of a strange kind disembarking from their ships on the sheltered beaches. These were buccaneers and pirates from various countries who regularly looted the coastal towns of South America and used the Galápagos as a hideout, as a place to carouse and stock their ships with the giant tortoises. During the following century increasing numbers of whalers sailed the waters around Galápagos. They too stopped frequently on the islands to load up their share of the diminishing tortoise population, as well as the fur seals, which they killed for their skins. Occasionally these people would settle on one of the islands, but none stayed very long, and it was not until later in the nineteenth century that colonists established themselves in a permanent way.

Long before this, however, an unusual small ship came to cruise the Galápagos for five weeks.

It was only twenty-seven meters long and carried over seventy men. Coming from England around Cape Horn, it was sailing on a four-year investigative journey around the world, and on board was a naturalist named Charles Darwin. He was an effervescent young man who was later to become one of the most prominent figures in the world of science. Along the coast of South America he had collected a tremendous wealth of knowledge in every field of natural history, and when he arrived in the Galápagos he did not fail to observe the incredible forms of animals that lived only there. He pondered their similarities and differences, and later he used some of them as evidence for his new theory of evolution.

Much was taken from this land before anyone came to appreciate the great beauties it contained. It had been a world in balance, where each individual animal and plant had developed an ability to survive in the harsh environment. The exquisitely delicate equilibrium was something to marvel at. But for the early men of the sea, survival was hard. They took a lot, often ruthlessly and irreparably, but much was left. Today a great many descendants of those animals that were neither aggressive nor fearful still roam the islands or scan the ocean for food and raise their own descendants.

Giant Tortoises on a Volcano

As I traveled to the different islands, I began to discover the great wild places where nature's rhythm still swung its slow pace among gentle colonies of active animals. I had long been familiar with the giant tortoises of Santa Cruz Island. Those that remained lived in the high, humid parts of the island, a forlorn group huddled here and there in the dense vegetation. Feral pigs preyed on their eggs and young, and human settlers occasionally made inroads into the remaining population. Two thousand still existed, but they were shy and dispersed and it was rare to see one feed, for the slightest human scent or sight would immediately make it drop its heavy body to the ground and retract its head and feet into the carapace with a long hissing exhalation.

One of my very favorite places in Galápagos is Volcan Alcedo, the central volcano of the long chain of five great shields forming Isabela Island, where the largest population of giant tortoises, numbering three or four thousand, still lives in relative safety. The first time I landed on the small black lava beach at the base of the dormant volcano a great feeling of anticipation filled me. A pale, smooth plain spread before me, slowly rising toward the interior, dotted sparsely with a few tufts of dry grass. Beyond, the rim of the volcano stood clear in the afternoon sky, carved sinuously by innumerable little ravines that predicted a humid and lush green summit. The ground consisted of a thick layer of gray pumice, which contrasted sharply with the usual dark, rocky coastal landscape. The small expedition that my father and I had been invited to join had traveled all day and part of the night from our home in Academy Bay. We had followed the low shores of Santa Cruz in total darkness, then skirted the tall lichen-covered cliffs of Pinzon Island. The little landing beach at Alcedo bore no name. In the boulders at both sides chocolate-colored fur seals called to one another in their eerily human voices, and before the sun sank over the mountain a small group of tiny Galápagos penguins passed by us offshore.

The next morning before daybreak we began our ascent. The beach was silent now and the air still as we walked single file up the flank of the volcano. The sun grew hot later that morning, as it always does in the warm season, and we seemed to get no closer to the rim of the volcano and its vast caldera. But as we advanced, the vegetation became more abundant, and many small birds—finches, mockingbirds, and flycatchers—flitted among the foliage. We finally arrived at the top toward midday. At over one thousand meters elevation the air was loaded with humidity, yet the caldera was clear of any clouds. The view dropped steeply, about three hundred meters down to the broad flat floor of the huge crater, which stretches seven kilometers across to the opposite wall to enclose this strange, circular world. The rim was quite green and overgrown with vegetation, and so were the flanks of the caldera wall; but toward the center of this vast pit the terrain was arid and only coastal-zone trees grew. We could see large patches of black lava where relatively recent eruptions had risen through fissures in the crater floor. The intermingling songs of a thousand finches below us were carried up sporadically by the breeze. The volcano measures more than twenty kilometers across its base at sea level, but just then it seemed infinitely broader. Behind us the tan-colored pumice plain extended unbroken to the distant white fringe where it met the ocean, and farther away still, on the horizon, lay another volcanic island, Santiago. Off in the distance, far to one side, we could hear the rhythmic groan of a male giant tortoise mating, while a few of these tranquil reptiles slept away the heat of the day under shady bushes. Later they moved out to feed, grazing the already well cropped grass around the short trees. In contrast with the shy tortoises I had known on Santa Cruz, they moved about unconcerned by our presence, munching with their sharp toothless jaws at every variety of plant they encountered. When they saw our gear, however, they appeared to be most intrigued. They sniffed and trampled it, and before their inquisitiveness was satisfied, they chewed on it with tremendous force. Eventually we had to build a fence of fallen logs around our tent to safeguard it from their destructive curiosity.

To the north of our camp rose the two huge domes of the other volcanoes of Isabela—Darwin and Wolf—which are separated by a vast low stretch of scorched black lava that forms a long saddle between them. Volcan Wolf, the northernmost volcano on the island, marks the highest point in the archipelago, about seventeen hundred meters. As we moved along the narrow rim surrounding the caldera, the volcanoes to the south also came into view. From here we could see where the eastern and western shores of the island form the Perry Isthmus at the foot of Alcedo. Beyond it, across further expanses of barren lava, the dark silhouette of Sierra Negra rises gradually, and barely discernible to the west, Cerro Azul stands in a blue haze, nearly as tall as Volcan Wolf.

All five volcanoes are quite active and through frequent eruptions have been constantly adding new lava flows to their structure, increasing their imposing mass. Not long ago they must have stood as five individual islands separated by narrow channels of sea, which since have been filled in by the dark young lava flows. Nonetheless, the rugged surface of these terrains still acts as an insurmountable barrier to the giant tortoises, and to the present time each volcano has retained its own race or subspecies of these ancient reptiles. Most of these populations have suffered great destruction from humans and from the introduced animals, and the race on Alcedo is the only one not endangered. Most feral mammals have not succeeded in crossing the low saddles; only donkeys and house cats roam the slopes in a wild state, but they seem not to seriously threaten the tortoises.

Fog rolled in on us, and as we walked deeper into the tortoise country of Volcan Alcedo, I was saddened to consider the irreversible destruction humans carry with them everywhere. I was embarrassed and ashamed to be one of my own kind. I saw a delicate spider web filled with dew drops and tried to avoid it, feeling that as an alien I did not have the right to demolish it, but I only fell into another I had not noticed. It was hopeless; I was an intruder. I watched the tortoises walk to and fro, drinking and wallowing in small fog drip puddles beneath moss-laden trees. They were not aware of what I represented to their kind and I was glad of that. Their shells glistened as it began to drizzle, and as I advanced, they successively appeared and disappeared in the fog on both sides of the winding wild donkey path.

By midafternoon we arrived above a boiling, roaring geyserlike pond nestled along the thickly overgrown inner slope of the caldera, a vivid reminder of Alcedo's active interior. In an adjacent little clearing we set up camp for the night, the wind now and again sweeping the warm and damp sulfurous vapors over us. The low clouds, which had grown menacingly dark, suddenly broke into a torrential rain. Thunder echoed in the caldera and rivulets streamed through our camp, forming small ponds in every depression.

This visit in 1969 marked the last time I would see the geyser bubbling and boiling through its pond of gray steaming water. Whether because of low rainfall or increased heat within the volcano, the following year it dried out completely, leaving only a roaring steam vent at the bottom of a small explosion crater. For several years we expected further activity from the volcano, but it has remained quiet, the billowing jet of superheated steam rising steadily into the air. Because it no longer resembled a true geyser, we began to refer to it simply as the steam vent. There are many other small fumaroles on Alcedo, and on cold mornings steam can be seen rising in innumerable places from the porous pumice ground among the vegetation. In certain locations sulfur fumes escape from small fissures and holes between boulders, accumulating around them delicate formations of bright yellow crystals.

I returned to Alcedo many times since that first visit, so many that I have lost count, and occasionally I stayed there for as long as two weeks with my family. During the warm rainy season everything is at its most beautiful. Below the steam vent a series of elongated plains stretches on the crater floor at the base of the inner wall. These are on the southern side, and since wind and rain predominate from this direction, they change drastically from a parched dusty brown area to lush green fields in a matter of a few weeks. The rainy season often starts suddenly and once I witnessed the first shower in what had obviously been a long time strike the volcano in full force.

We had walked along the rim the way we usually did to reach the area of the steam vent on the south side. The soil was dusty dry, save for some small muddy puddles resulting from the fog that became trapped and dripped from the thick coats of dark liverworts and other epiphytes that envelop the branches of prominent trees. Hundreds of tortoises had gathered on this higher part where the mist condensed more frequently. The air was crisp but above the outer flank of the volcano a few dark clouds had accumulated. As we descended into the caldera, the weather quickly changed and soon water was cascading down as if the skies had burst. At once tortoises all around us hurried out of the nearby bushes and converged in a few low spots that, from past experience, they knew would serve as water holes. They reached these areas before the water had time to collect and they drank out every little pocket as it accumulated. A few younger tortoises clambered onto a large smooth rock where the rain ran into a couple of small hollows; again they emptied the pool and waited for more rain to fall. Through thousands of years of such use, the rock had become shiny and polished, like a perfect stone dish.

In the plains of the caldera extensive ponds had formed. In a few days millions of seedlings had sprouted and the surroundings rapidly turned into a meadow, while tortoises from adjacent woodlands moved in and migrated down from the rim. The three-hundred-meter descent would not take the tortoises more than a day or two, and in ever increasing numbers they congregated around the water holes and grazed the tender green grass. In this Galápagos springtime their activity quickly reached a peak. They moved about busily, feeding a good part of the time and drinking enormous amounts of water while wallowing in the muddy pools. Mating was common throughout these days and so was aggression. Two individuals would encounter each other, raise their forelegs as high as they could, stretch their necks upward, and make a threatening display with their sharp gaping jaws. After a few moments the shyer one of the two, either male or female, would retreat and resume grazing nearby, so that such meetings never ended in a battle. The tortoises traveled about a great deal, often clambering up and down steep hillocks without altering their steady pace, and sometimes they made straight up toward the rim despite their considerable weight, which can reach six hundred pounds or so in large males.

Once in a while a strange encounter of great significance would occur. A tortoise might be grazing nonchalantly in the natural pasture or resting under a shady bush when a small Darwin's finch would alight directly before it. There the bird would hop around actively for a few seconds, until the great reptile raised its carapace high off the ground on outstretched legs, extending its head and neck backward over its shell. Recognizing the signal, the little bird would immediately set to work picking off ticks that bother the tortoise, submitting every fold of the leathery reptilian skin to a careful scrutiny. The tortoise would remain in this rigid position for as long as the cleaning procedure lasted, relieved temporarily of the obnoxious parasites as the finch obtained rich protein from the blood they contained.

The day of the tortoise is gentle and without urgency. Many a morning begins with a sleepy blanket of fine clouds covering the caldera floor. In the stillness beneath, the tortoises move about slowly at first, waiting for the sun's warmth to become fully active. They start feeding near the muddy wallows where many of them have spent the night. As the sun rises over the rim, its rays penetrate the cloud bank and rapidly disseminate it into the bright morning air, revealing a scene of increasing activity. Now the tortoises move about, grazing the tender herbs and short grass everywhere, and the mating groans uttered by the huge males echo from many directions. By midmorning they gradually head for the shade of shrubs and small trees while still feeding. At noon calm again prevails in the green clearings, for the tortoises could easily overheat and die if they were to remain in the blazing sun. A tortoise sleeps away the heat in the most relaxed of positions, limbs lying neglected on the ground, head outstretched or resting comfortably on one stubby foreleg. When the afternoon grows cooler, they begin a second foraging period, slowly returning to the ponds and puddles to drink large amounts of water. Here they bathe and wallow with great delight, churning the bottom ooze with a rotating motion of their bodies. For reasons not fully understood, many of the larger tortoises remain here to sleep. Perhaps it is for the accumulated warmth that the thick mud provides through the cool night, or for protection against the bothersome ticks, or a combination of the two. At any rate there is much shoving and pushing in these ponds at sunset. Some large individuals purposefully ram others, bulldozerlike, with the front of their carapace, while smaller tortoises are forced out of the water by rule of size as space is taken up. Tranquility begins to fill the atmosphere at the approach of the cool, moist night. Most young tortoises and females, which are smaller than the males, seek sleeping locations of their own. Where the soil is soft, they scrape out a nestlike form that they can settle into with maximum possible surface contact with the earth for warmth. At the first light of dawn they appear immobile, like so many boulders sitting in the unstirred water, dew trickling down their domed, shiny black backs. Many times I have watched the slow awakening of these ancient cold-blooded animals. How many such days had they seen emerge? How many seasons had they witnessed in the primeval world of their volcano home? Did they really live 150 or 200 years as we might believe?

As the rains start to subside, the water in the pools recedes rapidly and the air temperature drops slightly. The volcano is once again overtaken by drought, though fog will often envelop it. Then the rhythm of life slows down. Most of the tortoises move out of the open areas into the bushes, where they nibble on what greenery there is, or onto the rim of the volcano where mist and drizzle maintain a much higher degree of humidity than on the crater floor.

On one morning, as I watched the steam curl around the massive dark figures in the water, two females wandered leisurely out of the pool into the fine mist. They were easily recognizable by their medium size and smooth, rounded dome shells, polished and worn by the great concave plastron and rough forelegs of the mating males. They explored thoroughly a meadow of sparse low herbs covered with a weaving of dew-laden spider webs that shimmered in the early sunlight, and then they moved to a more vegetated area to begin feeding. In a couple of months, when drought once again invaded the crater, these same two females would start out on their slow, silent trip to the nesting grounds. The most important site lay at the very opposite side of the caldera floor, at the foot of the northern wall. There, each would select a spot of soft soil to dig a nest cavity where she would lay about a dozen round, hard-shelled eggs. This fantastic reptile, using only the blunt nails of her hind feet, knows how to excavate a perfect round hole. And perfect it is, requiring many hours of work, though she never turns to look at her own nest until it is properly covered with a layer of dirt. The area chosen is not so exposed to the mist and the eggs are incubated over a period of four to six months by the filtered warmth of the sun. The tiny, fragile young are ready to hatch with the arrival of a new rainy season. They dig their way out of the dry ground with needle-sharp claws designed for the purpose. For a long time they remain in the more arid parts of the caldera and it may be several years before they appear in the lush grazing areas of the adults. It is not until they are perhaps twenty-five years old that they in turn will begin reproducing, thus completing a new generation.

Several hundred thousand years ago tortoises very much like these roamed over many continents of the world. Their slow reproduction did not allow for rapid evolutionary changes or adaptations, and with mounting pressures from the many predators, they became extinct on the continental land masses. Before this happened, however, a few of the primeval tortoises had reached the Galápagos islands. Perhaps they had traveled as tiny tortoises on a natural raft of tangled vegetation, or perhaps they simply floated in from the sea, for they are quite buoyant and the currents could carry them to the islands in only one or two weeks. At any rate what they found suited them rather well, and they have changed very little over the many thousands of years since, just enough to form different types adapted to the varying habitats of the high and humid islands or the low and dry ones. A similar population, relict of times long past, can still be found on what is almost an antipode of Galápagos, Aldabra Island in the Indian Ocean, where the tortoises resemble the Galápagos giants so closely that they could easily be mistaken for them by an untrained observer.

On Alcedo I have followed the gentle giants out of their muddy pools and observed them as they feed, ingesting large amounts of unchewed grass and weeds. They are well adapted to grazing with their dome-shaped shells, their short necks and forelegs. With insular variations, this is the type that prevails on islands exceeding six hundred meters in elevation, where there are humid, green highlands with much low vegetation. On low, arid islands another form occurs, the saddleback, which has a long neck and slender legs, and a high raised fore edge of shell that enables them to reach high into the dry shrubbery and up to the hanging pads of tree cacti.

The Browsing Tortoise

The saddleback tortoises have been even more severely destroyed by man than the dome types, because their home islands, being smaller and lower, were repeatedly raided by hungry sailors of the past. The only population that now numbers more than one hundred adults is found on Pinzon, which is a centrally located island, an old volcano covered with dense, arid bush. Saddlebacks are smaller than dome types, but the conformation of the shell, neck, and forelegs enables them to reach astonishing heights while foraging. These tortoises are also quite different in attitude, for they walk briskly with long strides and are very alert. To watch an old male browsing near our camp I had to stalk him carefully through the bushes. If I stepped down heavily, he would feel the vibration in the ground; if I placed myself upwind, he would sniff the air, pumping his throat; and of course if I was anywhere in sight, he would raise his head to examine me suspiciously and eventually turn and move in the other direction. When I finally outstayed him by sitting quietly behind a clump of plants, he began eating heartily and the technique he used was a spectacle I will never forget.

He stationed himself beneath one of the many native croton shrubs, and slowly raised his head to sniff first one twig and then another. He did not seem to care for the leaves, but examined the base of the thin branches, which were about the thickness of a pencil. He ripped one of these sprigs with the toothlike tip of his jaw and pulled it down suddenly to break it, clawing clumsily with one of his stubby feet. Bypassing many lower limbs of the small tree, he lifted one front leg to gain an extra inch in height, balancing his bulky body on three legs, much as African elephants do to tear down the branches of some large tree. Once the old tortoise had accumulated enough food on the ground, he began eating at leisure, consuming leaves and sticks alike and repeating the process whenever he ran out. This seemed a very intelligent system for what we like to call a primitive reptile. Later I measured his maximum reach at 1.4 meters above the ground.

As I watched him eat the dry leaves and woody branches I noticed many signs of his old age. In addition to his large size, his shell was worn quite smooth and marked with long scratches left by stiff thorns and sharp rocks. He showed no growth ridge along the plates of his shell, and the thin leading margin above his neck was notched and chipped where he had rammed into boulders and tree trunks during his meanderings over the rocky terrain. Moving about, he discovered a small puddle of water in the hollow of a rock, left by the night's drizzle. He drank it out avidly, resumed feeding for a moment, then returned to the rock to obtain a few last drops. I thought how much easier life was for the dome-shaped tortoises of the wetter islands. On Alcedo there is always abundant vegetation in certain areas, compared to this arid island, and fog drip and drizzle collect in small puddles almost all year round.

Fringe of Life

To the west of Alcedo another massive island rises—the single enormous active volcano of Fernandina—where another race of tortoises once lived years ago. There are no accounts of early sailors having taken any for meat; the bare, rugged lava coast of the island is not a suitable place to conduct tortoise-gathering expeditions. Yet only one tortoise has ever been seen there, collected by a scientific party in 1906, the largest saddleback tortoise ever found. Little did the hardy scientist who killed it on the slope of the great volcano know that he would be the only man to see this race alive. Its extinction can probably be attributed to a cataclysmal eruption of this ponderous volcano.

Sometimes we sail to the dark shores of this island and explore among its strange inhabitants. One occasion will always remain vivid in my mind. We left the small black beach at the foot of Alcedo just before sundown and for most of the night we sailed under a full moon north along the eastern coast of Isabela. Whitecaps raced alongside and the dark red sails swayed gently against a background of a million stars. The great volcanoes of northern Isabela, Darwin and Wolf, dropped behind in the clear, crisp night, then reappeared as we passed them again on their western side, having rounded the island's northernmost tip. They stood high and cloudless in monochrome splendor, their recent lava flows distinctly visible as dark streaks among patches of paler vegetation. As we arrived at Punta Espinosa, the only safe anchorage on the island, Fernandina loomed somberly over us, an imposing symmetrical mass. Dawn was approaching, and the sinking moon nearly touched the shoulder of the great solitary volcano.

In this western part of the archipelago a particular climatic condition prevails. A cold deep sea current coming from the west upwells on encountering the land mass, bringing distinctly cold waters from the deep. These waters also carry rich nutrients to the surface, allowing marine organisms to reproduce in great numbers. Plankton thrive there and a luxuriant growth of algae covers the rocks in the shallows. Where the great form of the Fernandina volcano pierces the surface of the sea, this abundance of life reaches its very maximum. The shore itself is quite rugged and bare, like the flanks of the volcano made of long expanses of heaped and cracked lava fields of varying ages, many of them quite recent. In a narrow strip along the very edge of the ocean strange cold- and warm-blooded animals make their home, all of them depending directly or indirectly on the resources from the sea for their survival. The tiny Galápagos penguins leave every morning at dawn on their daily fishing trips, braying like foghorns, and bizarre, furry-looking flightless cormorants nest just above the high-water mark. Even the endemic rice rat, one of the very few land mammals of the Galápagos, makes its living here. A bold little rodent, it manages to survive off the meager food supplied by the scanty vegetation and from the debris that washes up on the beach. Most special of all, marine iguanas thrive by the thousands on the rich algae growth abounding in the shallows. They appear to be strewn everywhere along the shore, where they gather in dense groupings to rest in the sun.

One May I spent two weeks with my parents and brother at the westernmost tip of the island, Cape Douglas. Every night we slept out on the sandy beach. Inquisitive rice rats scratched in our hair, while courting penguins brayed through the dark stillness. Often we awakened to mornings of quiet, cool fog, typical of these cold waters, and found pairs of little webbed penguin tracks on the beach around us, where they had searched for adequate rocky slabs under which to build their nests. During the day they fished close offshore, sometimes in large numbers, and splashing fights occasionally broke out. Marine iguanas were everywhere, tightly covering boulders where fur seals dozed in the shade. Their jagged immobile outlines intermingled with the sharp lava; they overlapped one another's backs indifferently, so crowded were their extraordinary assemblages. Now and again a briny spray squirted into the air from their nostrils; their well-developed nasal glands eliminate excess salt in this fashion, permitting the iguanas to live entirely on seawater. Bright red and orange sally light-foot crabs meandered among the iguanas in search of edible tidbits, and tiny lava lizards flitted with great agility among the motionless iguana heads, snapping up flies. Every day at low tide these iguanas would move one by one slowly to the water's edge and cast themselves into the surf. Swimming with a steady undulation of their body and tail, they would advance a certain distance out to sea where they began diving to the bottom for their daily food. When they returned, the waves and current threw them about, beating them against the rocks before they could grab hold with their sharp claws and haul themselves, exhausted, onto dry land again.

In May the hatching season for the young iguanas approaches. About four months earlier many females had dug shallow burrows in the black lava sand above the tide line and buried their one to three soft-shelled, elongated eggs within. Incubated by the sun in the same manner as the giant tortoise eggs, the young iguanas would soon be ready to emerge into the world and begin a life of their own by the sea. This is a time of high predation by seabirds and by the Galápagos snakes that lurk in the shady cracks of the lava.

Along the rocky shore, among the iguanas, sally light-foot crabs, and seals, flightless cormorants dozed in the sun, their small ragged wings extended to dry. They were as dark as their surroundings except for the single note of color in their turquoise-blue eyes. Offshore, whales spouted frequently and porpoises leaped. Audubon shearwaters fed in huge flocks along with brown noddy terns and schools of tuna.

Inhabitants of a Caldera

Turning inland from the shore, the visitor confronts a sharply contrasting picture. Indeed, the landscape has the aspect of a baked, lifeless desert. For long distances black, cracked, heaped, and toppled lava flows succeed one another. Only rarely is there a patch of older terrain, missed by youthful lavas, that sustains some vegetation. After our stay at Cape Douglas we decided to travel on to the summit of the volcano and explore its huge caldera. We departed early one morning, heading across the bare lava fields to the interior. The sun soon rose above the mountain, beating down on the black surface until the air all around vibrated with rising heat waves, giving the illusion of movement in the distance. We progressed slowly but steadily in the heat, up a dry ravine that made walking easier, and onto the steeper slope that preceded the summit plateau. On both sides strings of scoria and spatter cones ran in straight lines up the flank, following the radial fissures of the volcano. The entire terrain was covered with a pale gray dusting of volcanic ash. This layer became thicker as we advanced until, where the ground leveled out again in the summit area, it blanketed every mound and depression evenly, concealing lava flows and rounding out every detail of the topography. It was the result of Fernandina's greatest recent volcanic event, which took place in 1968. A titanic explosion projected a huge cloud of ash high into the atmosphere. Where the cloud drifted to the west with the wind, it deposited a heavy coating several feet thick, smoothing the land and obliterating all forms of life in the area. At the same time the floor of the caldera collapsed, sinking into the volcano's complicated inner structure. In a matter of two weeks the caldera floor sank three hundred meters, increasing its former depth by one half.

After crossing a short stretch of level ground, we arrived at the edge of this fantastic caldera, which engulfed most of the summit plateau of the volcano and dropped nearly a thousand meters to a deep mineral-blue lake. The walls of the oval caldera were approximately four to six kilometers in diameter, and they appeared so sheer as to be nearly vertical. Here we camped for many days in the dry, crisp air typical of Fernandina's lofty rim. Every morning offered a scene of profound beauty. The first colors of the day arrived in the east, increasing steadily as the distant sun illuminated the atmospheric layers far above. Below, darkness prevailed, as if the caldera had trapped a piece of night within its steep rock walls, and strands of mist hung motionless in the dim light. When the sun rose, it proceeded to explore these sheer escarpments, its warm rays creeping slowly into the abyss to reveal every detail, every crevice, and every layer of prehistoric lava. In the rocky rubble accumulated at their base the light picked up the fine white plumes of the fumaroles, whose steam rose vertically in the still air. This heat would often create shredded balls of cloud, which hovered above them, whirling and contorting as they condensed and evaporated in a continuous sequence. Finally, nearly two hours after it had first appeared, the sunlight plunged into the quiet mineral-laden lake, which shimmered and sparkled as the first wisps of the daily breeze agitated its surface. It was almost circular and extended nearly two kilometers from shore to shore.

Wherever vegetation grew on the ashfall, and especially along the north and east rim where ash and lava had not disturbed the dense greenery, yellow-orange land iguanas roamed like prehistoric dragons. They were bulky creatures, stout and muscular, their heavy bodies supported on sturdy, clawed legs and their backs covered with a crest of blunt yellow spines. The head of the land iguana presents an intricate pattern of reptilian scales, forming an extremely efficient protection. They dig roomy burrows in the ash or live in natural small lava caves, several females often sharing this home with one male. Being vegetarian, they feed on many types of plants, but have a special liking for the fallen pads of *Opuntia* cacti.

These iguanas appear on other islands as well, but on many they have been seriously reduced or even exterminated by introduced cats and dogs. Here on Fernandina they thrive, for there are no introduced animals, and their habitat is untouched. In the morning we watched them as they emerged everywhere from their underground dwellings, more and more of them, until there were iguanas feeding around every clump of plants. Big males with rusty red blotches on their sides nodded their heads in aggression and females were chased by larger rivals. Land iguanas are territorial and combats sometimes broke out between antagonistic males. Thoraxes inflated, mouths half open, and heads lowered, they lurched at each other again and again, trying to get a grip on the other's neck or flank with their powerful jaws. With legs arched and muscles flexed, they lean against each other, until after many hours one retreats, exhausted.

Little Darwin's finches have established a symbiotic relationship with the iguanas on Fernandina by eating the ticks from them, and like the giant tortoises, the iguanas raise their bodies off the ground to allow the small birds to clean them thoroughly.

Day after day the ominous sight of the deep caldera became more compelling, and toward the end of our two-week stay we decided to explore its floor and lake. The descent was precarious and impressively steep in many places, but when we reached the lake shore we were overwhelmed by the fantastic atmosphere provided by the serene, silent surroundings and the tall rock wall that encircled us, awesome reminders of the great volcanic pit within which we were dwarfed and insignificant. The lake water was not fit to drink, for it was laden with mineral salts, but life proliferated here in astonishing abundance. Myriads of small insects reproduced in the water and as many dragonflies and their larvae preyed upon them. Several hundred white-cheeked pintail ducks also made their living off these aquatic riches. In the morning stillness they paddled about with their downy young, pecking tiny insects off the mirror surface of the lake, intrigued by our unexpected presence in a world where humans are very rarely seen.

Nights here were even calmer than on the rim and considerably warmer. In the immense silence we were occasionally awakened by the ominous sound of a large rock avalanche rumbling down the unstable wall. Against the grinding sound of hundreds of tons of disintegrating stone, we could hear the explosive impact of huge boulders gaining speed and bouncing along the steep talus slope, sometimes landing in the lake with a loud splash. The free-falling rocks whistled through the air, and their echo lingered in the caldera. But even these spontaneous landslides resulting from the volcano's instability did not succeed in disrupting the profound tranquility that prevailed in this bizarre world.

Volcanic Eruptions

In 1977 I returned to the caldera of Fernandina. The reason for this visit was that lava had begun pouring into the lake from a fissure along the inner wall of the crater.

The eruption began before dawn one morning, and two days later word that Fernandina was active again reached Academy Bay, thanks to seismographic recordings and the report of a scientist who had just returned from a field trip to that island. Immediately an expedition was assembled to collect all the geological information that could be gleaned from the event, and I was fortunate to be chosen as one of the four participants. Sailing at sunrise from Academy Bay, we traveled for a long twenty-two hours on a mirror-calm sea, rounding the southern volcanoes of Isabela during the night before disembarking with our heavy packs and water reserve on the familiar shore of Fernandina. At once we began our long, hot scramble to the top and we arrived at the rim of the caldera sometime after nightfall. Although strands of mist drifted over the old ashfall, the caldera was clear of clouds, but to our disappointment no red glow emanated from its opposite wall where the lava had run in molten streams only a few days earlier. However, in the faint light we could see that a large new delta of lava had accumulated at the base of the wall and extended well into the lake. In the days that followed, we explored as much as we could of this terrain that was only a few days old. We climbed down to the new eruptive crevice and found that, except for the hot air that escaped from the gaping vents, it was almost identical to the older but still unchanged small cones that dot the outer flanks of the volcano. When we descended to the caldera floor we discovered that because of the tremendous rise in lake temperature from the enormous input of molten lava, the water still read a consistent 39 °C. (102 °F.). In the early morning before the wind rose, we rowed across the lake to the foot of the bleak new lava tongue in a small inflatable raft that had been brought here by a geological expedition. Steam was rising steadily from the edge of the lava, and as we approached, the thermometer we were dragging in the water began to climb steadily, reaching 45 °C. (113 °F.) where we landed and 80 °C. (176 °F.) at the edge of the new delta. The air was silent and peaceful, and only the turbulent whirls and loops of the ascending water vapors attested to the great activity that had taken place less than two weeks earlier. The paroxysm had subsided, but the lake water had become so heated that all its microorganisms had perished. Pintails still paddled along the shore, but because they found no food, they too were beginning to die. Having known no other world than their caldera home for several generations, they were now starving—their limited experience gave them no incentive to fly to another island. Such is the marginal existence led by the little inhabitants of a live volcano.

As the last words in this book were being written, one more such adventure suddenly transported us from Academy Bay back to the wilds of this volcano. It happened without warning; late one afternoon a friend dropped in to tell us that Fernandina's volcano was erupting again. Bits of news had arrived by radio from some of the tourist boats that were in the vicinity of the island. Still longing after many years to witness a volcanic eruption in full action, we jumped to our feet, rushed to buy provisions, filled our packs, refueled our boat, and were heading westward by eleven o'clock that night. The next morning at three I found myself sitting at the helm, still wearing the skirt I had on when the news had broken, instead of my usual shorts. A cool breeze filled our sails and speeded us toward the hidden shores of Isabela Island, our proud boat *Inti* slicing through the phosphorescent seas. Beneath the shredded low clouds a distant livid glow in the sky revealed the ongoing activity of Fernandina, still far away.

That day we rounded the southern tip of Isabela, and with the very last light of sunset dropped anchor at Punta Espinosa on Fernandina. It was too late to begin the climb, and we watched in awe the steamy-white contorting cloud that hung over the caldera, resulting from the heat caused by the eruption. As darkness gradually enveloped us, this cloud acquired a strange luminescence. Reflecting the light of the molten lava inside the caldera, it glowed more and more intensely in red tones of incredible richness.

We began our climb the next morning at sunrise on a calm and brilliantly clear day. Although we reached the summit within fifty-two hours of the onset of the eruption, the activity had already died down considerably. However, that night the fissure inside the caldera started to spew lava again. We sat in the darkness on the rim of the great crater, watching the activity awaken. Over the fierce wind I could hear our concerted whoops each time the fragments of molten lava were expelled more explosively out of the flaming vent. Like red-orange fireworks the fountains of lava spurted in graceful arcs, perhaps ten or fifteen meters into the air. Even though this was only a miniature eruption, I believe we were as fascinated as if we had been watching the greatest explosion man has ever witnessed.

We spent three more days observing the activity and living with the hawks and land iguanas in their lofty homeland. Before our arrival the fresh lava had run over two kilometers down to the caldera lake. This was now cooled and quite black, but the water was still steaming over its entire surface, and the little pintails must have died or fled. The route we had followed down to the lake shore the year before was now covered with jagged new lava.

Our last night on Fernandina was spent on the beach at Cape Douglas, among the braying penguins, the nesting cormorants, the sea lions, fur seals, and marine iguanas. The night was calm and the moon traveled placidly across the cloudless sky. The following day we passed along the other mighty volcanoes of Isabela on our way back home.

Little did I realize that a few months later I would again be hurrying up another volcano in my elusive pursuit of a full-scale volcanic eruption. This one took place on Cerro Azul, the southernmost volcano of Isabela. On February 1, 1979, a fissure about one kilometer long near the eastern base of this enormous volcano began disgorging lava in great spasmodic fountains as well as long, luminous rivers. When I arrived at the site ten days later the brilliantly glowing lava was shooting as much as two hundred meters into the air, accompanied by mighty roars and explosions. Millions of fragments of molten rock rose and fell like curtains of light in the night sky. Around two principal vents the glowing debris, descending in dense showers, had built ramparts almost a hundred meters high, forming cones that were growing and changing shape as more matter was being added. With each explosion the earth vibrated, and where we camped, a little over half a kilometer away, the radiated heat could be felt as if from the world's most gigantic bonfire. At night the entire surrounding landscape and sky above were bathed in an eerie red light, illuminating owls as they searched for rodents quite unperturbed. On one side the cones surrounding the vents were deeply breached and lava cascaded downslope like ribbons of fire as magma continued to rise. The fantastic activity rose and fell in paroxysms and lulls. The lava flows, cooling into great, jumbled black fields, reached perhaps ten kilometers in length.

Through three unbelievable evenings I sat, hour after hour, spellbound by this spectacle exploding before my eyes. For three whole weeks the volcano belched torrents of liquid lava and great jets of gas, then gradually the activity died away and Cerro Azul rejoined its neighbors in quiet, temporary, slumber.

From Island to Island

Chapter Four

Means of Transport

I have always been fascinated by the mighty shield volcanoes of Isabela and Fernandina and the special wildlife that these mountains shelter. Nonetheless, there are so many places of endless charm and beauty in the Galápagos that a lifetime does not seem long enough to explore them.

As a child I traveled with my parents to a few of the islands and bays close to our home in a small boat, the *Puck,* which my father had built the year after my brother was born. It was too small for us to live aboard, so we camped on shore every night. Later my parents sold this boat and acquired the *Kim,* with which we explored the Galápagos shores in detail, sailing ever farther from our home island and visiting places we had not even heard of. The *Kim,* only seven meters in length, was open and not very seaworthy, and as my brother and I grew older, the space on board became increasingly cramped.

Often we talked of how we would build another boat with our own hands, a true sailing ship that could take us around the world if we wished. Slowly we began accumulating lumber from the continent and copper wire from which we fashioned nails. My father collected nautical magazines and books and carefully drew a set of plans for a boat that would suit our purposes. To lay the keel, we melted two tons of lead in an iron barrel and poured it into a makeshift mold of wood and sheet metal. We then bolted it to beams hewn from a rare local wood, extremely hard and almost indestructible in seawater. The frames grew slowly, fastened with hand-made nails, rivets, and wooden pegs. For years we planed, adjusted, and assembled, for almost everything had to be done by hand. Gradually the planking was fitted and the deck covered. We glued a hollow mast together and spliced the rigging, and finally on a bright, windy day in March 1976, in the middle of our loveliest season, the proud new *Inti* was launched. She was ten meters long and weighed four tons; with considerable effort we moved her a hundred meters from our workshop to the beach on planks and steel rollers, down to a spot where the incoming tide would lift her. There she stood, lapped by the waves for the first time, pointing into the stiff east wind. After many years of sacrifice and hard labor we were at last free to travel unhampered among our treasured islands.

During the years that our boat was in construction I had continued to travel, working occasionally as a guide for tourists cruising around the islands on yachts. This had allowed me to pay for my photography and to visit places I had not seen before. But now we would be able to move at will or stay in one spot for as long as our interest lasted. We could also sail to the outlying islands without feeling threatened by bad weather along the way.

Profoundly tranquil feelings overtake me aboard our boat at sunset when the sea is calm, as I watch the departure of the swallow-tailed gulls for their nightly forays. The grace of their shape and movements is ever so perfect as they drift one by one over our mast and on to the dimming horizon. The last glow of sunshine catches their immaculate plumage, while the pale blue sky can be seen through their delicate wing feathers. As darkness falls, schools of small fish become visible in the phosphorescent glow of myriad planktonic organisms, and I try to imagine the gulls silently snatching their prey from the surface. And when the sky begins to regain its color after the long night of cruising, having watched the stars and our luminescent wake, or listened to porpoises leap from the crest of dark waves, again I can discern small groups of swallowtails appearing in the hazy light, this time gliding back to shore.

An Island of Seabirds

One of our first trips took us to Tower Island, the northeasternmost of the Galápagos group. Its remote location makes it a prime nesting ground for the many birds that spend most of their lives fishing over vast stretches of unbroken ocean. Here hundreds of thousands of these oceanic birds converge for the sole purpose of reproducing their kind.

The long sail to Tower took us completely out of sight of land before we spotted a low gray streak barely breaking the horizon, like a wedge between air and sea. The island consists of an enormous inactive volcano, of which only the very summit protrudes above water. It has two large calderas: the one in the center is filled with a salt-water lake, and the other to the south side forms Darwin Bay. Already we noticed a great number of seabirds flying above us. Some were leaving the island; others were returning in flocks to the shore and their nests. Young boobies inspected the rigging of our ship with great curiosity, while tiny storm petrels flitted about the crests of jagged waves. Sea currents are swift around the undercut cliffs of Tower, and it is often a struggle to enter the calm waters of Darwin Bay. As we left the long, rough passage behind, we felt at once entwined in this dizzying world of seabirds. Long strings of masked and red-footed boobies sailed in from the ocean to the hungry young that awaited them anxiously inland. Shimmering white swallow-tailed gulls turned and dipped gracefully along the dark cliffs that encircle the bay, and great frigate birds soared motionlessly everywhere. Above a small knoll a column of these birds slowly formed in a thermal updraft. In circles and loops they spiraled higher and higher, without seeming to move a feather until they disappeared one by one into the thin clouds.

On the island immaculate white-masked boobies form raucous colonies on the windward coast, while tens of thousands of pairs of slender red-footed boobies occupy the short silvery *Bursera* trees that cover the island. The pelagic red-billed tropic birds, with their gleaming plumage and long streaming tails, go through aerial displays before the lava cliffs, where they nest in deep hidden cavities, alongside the black and white Audubon shearwaters.

On the eastern point of land enclosing Darwin Bay nests a population of storm petrels that numbers perhaps half a million birds. Band-rumped storm petrels flutter from dawn until dusk in an almost soundless, feathery maze. Like dead leaves caught in a whirl of wind, they twist and turn tirelessly over the seaward cliffs, sometimes even colliding in the air. Occasionally one can be seen to disappear surreptitiously beneath a rock slab. If you listen carefully, you can hear the muted murmur of countless tiny birds as they secretly tend to their nests under the crusty lava. When the afternoon sun goes down, their numbers diminish gradually, and by nightfall another species, the wedge-rumped storm petrel, takes over the colony. Short-eared owls prey on them then, and in the oversized lava bubbles scattered feathery remains attest to the owls' nightly feast.

A third species of storm petrel, the white-vented, lives in the archipelago, but its nesting grounds have never been found. It can be seen closer to shore than its two other relatives, pattering in typical storm petrel fashion with its delicate small webbed feet on the surface of the sea, hovering like a butterfly, and picking up tiny organic debris and plankton for food.

Tenuous Life of the Great Frigate

Two species of frigate birds nest on Tower, the great and the magnificent. Both frigates are very similar; the males can be distinguished only by a difference in the metallic sheen of the feathers on their backs, and the females by the extent of white on their chests and a pink eye-ring instead of a blue one. Only a few hundred magnificent frigates nest on the island, whereas several thousand pairs of greats are scattered throughout. I had decided to record in photographs the fascinating details of the great frigate bird's life on this April trip, for I knew that this was the time when the frigates perform their stupendous courtship ritual.

Just beyond the small beach where we landed was a stretch of low salty bushes where a great number of male frigates concentrate for their courtship display. The males sit in small groups in the evergreen shrubs, and when a white-chested female appears soaring above them, the entire colony launches into an incredible display, ardently exposing their huge, air-filled scarlet throat pouches toward the sky. Uttering a concert of clear, cooing warbles, the great black birds throw their heads back, exhibiting the full size of their distended balloons and swiveling on their perches as the female passes overhead. Shimmering green scapular feathers flutter in the wind while the great outstretched wings are shaken in violent vibrations. When a female descends and hovers over one male in the group, they all go into a frenzy. If she has made her choice, she will alight near one of them, ignoring the rest. They rub their heads and chests together and the male surrounds his new mate with his expanded wings. Yet sometimes the female will leave at this point and continue her search. If she stays, the pair drifts into the long courting ecstasy, building mutual trust and cementing the strong bond needed for the many months of hard work and parental devotion that lie ahead.

For many days on end the males will sit, unconcerned with food, sleeping fitfully with their heads resting on their wilted pouches, occasionally resuming their attempt to attract a prospective mate overhead. As the hubbub of display activity continues within the colony, those that have already formed pairs shift to a new occupation. The male's pouch slowly shrivels, losing its intensive color, and soon they will both begin the task of building a nest. For this the male makes dozens of trips every day, snatching twigs from shrubs and trees or picking up branches floating in the water with a masterly dive in full flight. Each time he quickly returns, cooing softly to his mate, who has remained on the display site, and presents her with the material. She arranges and assembles it into a fragile platform in preparation for the forthcoming egg. Once the single white egg has been laid, both birds share the fifty-five-day incubation. As their feeding trips are long and distant, each bird may take turns as long as two weeks in duration, sitting on the nest motionlessly day and night with no food or water, waiting faithfully for its mate to return.

The tiny chick hatches weak and helpless, blind and totally naked. Only after several weeks does it acquire a beautiful layer of white down, which resembles a soft blanket of cotton wool. Until this time it must be constantly shielded by its parents from the sun and from predation by other frigates and lava gulls. The parents take turns protecting it and make frequent trips to feed their growing offspring on partially digested, regurgitated fish.

The young frigate's growth is slow, for it is difficult to gather enough food to sustain such large birds. At the age of six months, the chick has lost its downy white and grown a black plumage with a white and rufous head. By now it has attained the size of its parents and can begin to fly. But food is still in short supply, and starvation is always a threat. It is very difficult for the immature chick to learn the highly specialized skills needed to catch flying fish on the wing far out at sea, as the adults do. As a result it will remain partially dependent on its parents for food during this learning period, at least six more months, and will return to the site of the now disintegrated nest to meet them. This means that a complete nesting cycle may last as long as sixteen or eighteen months, so that the successful adults can nest only every other year. Even at the end of this very long period, the juvenile frigate will have great difficulty adapting to the feeding techniques typical of its race, and many die of starvation before they are able to perfect them.

The great frigate is a pelagic bird and does most of its feeding far from land, swooping low over the crest of waves to flush flying fish into the air, and snatching them before they have time to dive again.

Another mode of feeding developed by certain frigates near the breeding colony is the pirating of other birds as they return from the sea to feed their own young. Many times I have observed a frigate soaring nonchalantly above the shoreline, then suddenly plunging in a tremendous burst of speed, as if transformed into a plummeting, feathered arrow, to attack an incoming booby. If the unfortunate booby has a gizzardful of fish he may quickly regurgitate and drop his catch to lighten his load and facilitate his escape. This, of course, is what the attacking frigate wants, and with an expert dive he usually intercepts the food before it reaches the ground. If the booby delays in relinquishing his fish, his pursuer may grab him by the tail and upend him to hasten the decision. The loudly squawking booby usually ends up falling into the water or shrubbery. Even though many frigates chase boobies and other seabirds, only certain individuals seem to develop the skill necessary to recognize a loaded booby from an empty one. The pirate frigates are for the most part adult males, and although their initial attack is made at random, they can decide in a few seconds whether to continue; if they do, they are immediately joined by a large flock of competitors in the swift and violent chases.

The flight of the frigate is a fascinating sight, for their aerial acrobatics are almost unreal. These agile scavengers swoop down with perfect precision, using their long hooked beaks to pluck the tiniest morsel off the surface of the water or beach. Midair squabbles frequently ensue, as food is almost always in great demand. In an audible rustle of feathers they tangle, vault, hover, and sometimes fly backwards until the swiftest one, eluding the pursuit, manages to bolt the mouthful. Unlike other seabirds, they never alight on the water, as their feathers could easily become waterlogged. Although they may dip head or body while feeding or bathing, they always keep their wings clear above the surface. The wingspan of a great frigate measures 2.4 meters (8 feet) and the average weight of an adult is about 1.4 kg. (3 pounds). All five species of frigate birds around the world boast the greatest wing surface ratio to body weight of any living bird, which may be the reason why they have become the grandest masters of the air ever to exist. Frigates are completely at ease only in flight, and they feed, fight, gather nesting material, bathe, and perhaps even sleep on the wing as they travel hundreds and sometimes thousands of kilometers away from land without touching down.

Two Very Special Gulls

On Tower Island also live two of the world's most special gulls. Both are unique to the Galápagos, yet they are totally different from each other. The lava gull is a strange species. Although it is very typical of gulls in being a coastal scavenger, it appears to occupy a marginal and inefficient position in the Galápagos ecosystem. It rarely breeds and seems to spend a good part of its time in small flocks loafing in tidal lagoons, where its social laughing calls can be heard late into moonlit nights. Only about four hundred of these birds inhabit the entire archipelago, and there is no indication that there were large numbers of them in the past. This is an extremely small natural population to represent all the members of a species. To this day only a handful of lava gull nests have been found and observed. This is all the more surprising since both parents violently attack all intruders larger than themselves, plunging from the air with aggressive calls and hitting the intruder's head with swift blows of their dangling feet. On the low, sandy little island of Mosquera I once watched a pair repeatedly drive away the numerous sea lions that approached their vulnerable nest in a patch of low succulent plants. Even after the young have fledged, adult lava gulls will remain with them, feeding and defending them for a few more weeks.

By contrast, around twenty thousand swallow-tailed gulls live on the islands. The volcanic sea cliffs of the Galápagos are their prime breeding places. As they soar along the dark lava faces, swiveling weightlessly in the humid sea wind, the sun gleams through their slender white wings and clearly forked tails. It is a dizzying experience to follow one of these birds as it floats on the sea breeze, circling, rising, and dropping on buoyant wingbeats, its elegant body quivering ever so lightly with the streams of air that carry it. For a moment it seems to be lacking in decision, swerving, hanging motionless over the cliff edge, and then swerving again. Occasionally it lets out a thin, shrill scream in response to others of its kind, then finally it descends to its nest on a narrow rocky edge. As it settles down, others depart and the motion continues. Its bright pink legs and feet are thin and fragile, its body slender, and its beak long and pointed. But the most remarkable feature is the huge black eyes enhanced by thin rings of bright orange skin, giving the bird a distinctly ungull-like appearance. Its alarm call, a harsh rattle followed by a thin scream uttered through widely open beak, is notable, as are its behavior and life cycle.

Unlike all other gulls, the swallowtails are nocturnal, feeding on fish and squid caught at sea, for which task their eyes are beautifully adapted. Daytime is usually quiet within the colony, for most birds sleep through the warmer hours. However, near dusk and dawn the activity mounts into an incessant chorus of screams, rattles, and croaks as territorial squabbles erupt and courtship displays intensify. Soon after sunset the swallowtails begin circling over the nesting area and, as evening becomes rapidly darker, they start to fly out to sea in small groups. By the time complete darkness has overtaken the colony the only birds remaining are those tending nests. In the hours after midnight mates return, relieving those that have stayed behind. All birds return before sunrise, feeding their young or resuming courtship activity.

Each female lays a single egg in a nest made from as many as several hundred small pebbles carried one by one to the site with considerable care. Both parents take turns incubating for a little over a month until the fluffy chick emerges, well protected in a thick layer of camouflage gray down. Even so, predation is high and many young are eaten by marauding short-eared owls and frigate birds, and sometimes even by the large red sally light-foot crabs common on every seashore. The parent gulls are relatively helpless at warding off such dangers; they scream pathetically in alarm but do not retaliate.

A successful chick grows steadily and may take his first hesitant flight over the cliff edge by the time he is two months old, although his parents will continue to feed him for another month. Then one night the adults leave and do not return. Whether the chick accompanies them or flies off in his own direction is not known. At any rate, the young gull will not be seen near land until he has reached full breeding plumage, which takes about three years. All nonbreeders migrate south and east, into the cold nutrient-rich waters of the Humboldt Current off the coast of Ecuador and Peru. They remain at sea for about four months and then return to the Galápagos to begin a new nesting cycle.

Dance of the Blue-footed Booby

Daphne Island is a small volcanic cone protruding from the sea in the lee of Santa Cruz Island. It rises smoothly above the water to about 180 meters, girdled by undercut cliffs and covered only with a very sparse blanket of shrubs and a few cacti. It is made of volcanic tuff and is marked by a steep-sided crater at its center. The floor of this pit is flat and sandy, and here a strange atmosphere of urgent activity prevails during the cooler months of the year. This is the time when food supplies are most reliable for the blue-footed boobies. Consequently several thousands of these strange and specialized seabirds converge here to nest.

On the edge of the crater I often sit and marvel at the intensity of life below, before the morning sun penetrates the bizarre world of this little caldron. In the shady coolness every free space is occupied by a pair deeply involved in elaborate courtship. A male sky-points with a long plaintive whistle, throwing his wings up in an almost impossible position, head and tail cocked vertically to attract the attention of a nearby female. As she draws near, he intensifies his sky-pointing, then shifts to a slow and meticulous dance. With his beak and tail held stiffly up in the air, he lifts his stupendous blue webs alternately in a slow, cadenced motion. The female soon joins him, intertwining her neck with his and sky-pointing simultaneously. Soon they proceed to present each other with symbolic nest-building materials, exchanging small pebbles, twigs, or feathers. Yet oddly enough, their nest will consist only of a shallow scrape in the ground, and their carefully chosen items will be scattered and unused. Everywhere on the crater floor the activity is feverish, while from the windless sky more boobies spiral down to join the gathering.

There is a sense of urgency in the courtship of the blue-footed boobies, for they begin nesting when food is in good supply, a situation that may change unexpectedly any day. Their mode of fishing in shallow water close to shore requires that the fish be abundant if their young are to be fed successfully. If the fish population moves too far from the colony, the birds will be forced to abandon their nesting effort altogether, even if it means leaving half-grown chicks to starve. Therefore the eggs, from the usual two to the rare maximum of four, are laid quickly. Even though they are produced over a period of a few days, the parents begin incubation with the arrival of the first egg. This means that the chicks hatch over a period of days, an age difference that can be seen throughout their development. If the food supply becomes critical, and the parents cannot bring enough fish for the entire brood, the younger, weaker chicks will die and only the largest ones will reach maturity. If the chicks were all of the same age, they would all die together, and no offspring at all would result in a lean year.

Once I witnessed the sad failure of an entire nesting colony. It was during our warmer months, between January and May, and the nesting was dependent on an untimely abundance of fish. Many pairs were caring for two or three large, well-fed young, while countless others were still at the peak of courtship. Two weeks later I returned and found that disaster had struck. In the deserted colony downy carcasses littered the ground; a few large chicks, unable to fly, waited listlessly for their parents. When a rare parent arrived, he was so fiercely assaulted by these desperate, starving young that he would fly off again before having had a chance to feed his own offspring. For a while the experience left me profoundly depressed, yet it is this fine line between life and death, success and failure, that keeps the boobies and all other living forms in balance with their surroundings. In a few weeks or months, I knew, the blue-footed boobies would be back again for another, probably more fortunate, attempt at breeding.

The booby's dive is both extraordinary and beautiful to watch. Despite its streamlined body and the air cushions that exist beneath its skin, I have yet to understand how this bird can withstand the impact of hitting water from a height of perhaps fifteen meters. The male blue-foot is markedly lighter than the female, weighing only two thirds of her average 1.8 kilos, and as a result has an incredible underwater maneuverability for chasing fish and avoiding obstacles. He can thus master the most breathtaking dives in less than one meter of water. The boobies' serrated bill allows them to catch and hold slippery fish with great efficiency; they almost always swallow their prey even before surfacing. While the red-footed and masked boobies feed at sea away from shore, the blue-foots are coastal and have greater versatility. Sometimes, rather than plunging vertically from the air, they will skim the surface and dive at high speed at a very low angle to catch surfacing fish, yet they will manage to maintain enough velocity to continue flying when they emerge from the water a meter or so away.

When huge schools of tiny fish occasionally concentrate in sheltered bays, hundreds or even thousands of blue-footed boobies may gather to benefit from the profusion. In vast clouds they attack the fry, and it is hard to understand how they avoid one another both in the air and under water. In a dizzying continuity they take off from the surface, gain enough height, then immediately drop again like rain—the sea is puckered by their nonstop impacts. This goes on until the fish dissipate for a while and the replete birds alight on the nearest rocks for a rest. After an hour or two the fish have regrouped and the frenzied diving begins again. Yet for most of their lives, the boobies scan the shallows alone or in groups of less than a dozen and have to work hard for their daily catch.

The Red-billed Tropic Bird

While the blue-footed boobies occupy the sheltered interior of the crater on Daphne Island, vociferous pairs of masked boobies tend to their fluffy young on the outer slope of this small volcano. Here too I have spent long hours observing the courtship flight of the red-billed tropic bird. Never altering their steady wingbeat, these extraordinary creatures circle again and again in small flocks. Every time they come close to land they let out a concert of ear-piercing screams, hold their wings stiffly in a V-shape for a few seconds, then resume their incessant turns. When they fly near enough I can see their gleaming black eyes, their daggerlike red bills, their long streaming white tails undulating. I have watched them plunge with great force into their nesting cavities among fissures and boulders, screaming to one another in an underground greeting display. One time I was fortunate enough to spend two days observing the comings and goings in an unusually well exposed nest and was able to imagine and reconstruct the private life of this secretive tropic bird.

With steady, rapid wingbeats, the sparkling white bird flies over the deep ocean. At this point he has already been traveling over the sea for many months, sometimes describing large vague circles and occasionally staying with pelagic schools of fish, but always alighting on the water when in need of rest. But now he is traveling in a straight line, as if determined to reach a specific place that very day. Perhaps the water temperature has changed imperceptibly, causing the fish to become abundant, and something within his body has told his instincts that he is ready to breed again. It has been almost a year since the tropic bird has been onshore. A few times he had distinguished the faint contour of an island in the distant haze, but it did not attract him or affect his wanderings. However, now he is progressing at great speed, although he cannot yet see that speck of land he knows to be beyond the horizon. He cocks his head from side to side, intent on a silvery motion beneath the surface of the sea. If he locates a fish or squid of the right size at the right depth, he will plunge vertically down, like the boobies, wings half closed and hitting the water with hardly a splash.

The first island comes into view, but the tropic bird avoids it and continues to move on. Finally he arrives at Daphne and, recognizing its familiar shape, he knows that he is home. Several others are already performing their display flight, and soon he joins them. First he finds a mate, and then he proceeds to select a suitable nesting cavity along the steep slope of the island.

As with other seabirds, a long and perilous job awaits the newly formed pair, that of successfully hatching and raising their offspring. Owls may kill and eat the chick and starvation is a constant threat to the adults who must trust each other completely to share equally their parental duties. Every day they must catch enough fish to sustain themselves and fill the demands of the rapidly growing young as well.

But another danger hangs over the weary tropic bird homing in on his nest: the pirating frigate. Accelerating to all the speed he can produce, he may try to elude it; but frigates are swift and rarely give up. If robbed, perhaps he will still have enough food to give his young, but more likely he will have to turn back to sea and start fishing anew.

Usually, however, the parents arrive at the nest unmolested. Each day the chick requires greater amounts of food as he grows heavier and stronger, and the soft purrs he used to emit when his parents returned have changed to loud peeps and screams. Gradually the woolly down that covered his plump body is replaced by an immaculate silky plumage. One day about two months after hatching, his parents do not come to feed him. He does not realize what has happened, so he merely waits. The adults, exhausted from weeks of marginal living, have left the area and headed out onto the ocean again. As the chick grows hungry, his instinct tells him he should leave too, so on a windy morning he opens his perfect new wings and pushes off the narrow ledge in front of the rock cavity that was his nest. Like the others of his kind, he moves toward the open ocean.

Hood Island Community

Tropic birds, frigates, blue-footed and masked boobies, and swallow-tailed gulls are also found on the southernmost Galápagos island, which is called Hood or Española. Yet a different and very special community exists here. Being upwind and upcurrent from the rest of the islands, Hood Island has experienced more species isolation, because of fewer island interchanges. As a result many of the animals on Hood have evolved into unique forms. The lava lizards there are a much larger species than elsewhere, as are the mocking-birds. The Hood marine iguanas are very slender and the males during the breeding season acquire bright red and copper-oxide green blotches on their backs and legs. Even the local race of tortoises, of which very few remain, are the most extreme type of saddlebacks.

Perhaps the most spectacular inhabitant of Hood Island is the waved albatross. It is a stately bird with a wing span of 2.4 meters, making it a superb flier, as are all albatrosses. The waved albatross has a long, slender yellow beak, an immaculate white neck, and small wavy lines on its breast that give the bird its name. Tufted white feathers on its brows shade deep black eyes, accentuating the intensity of its stare.

Every year the waved albatross appears near the island in March or April. The first birds to arrive can be seen circling above the dark cliffs for hours. Then, one by one they alight in the rocky clearings among scrubby vegetation. As more come in from their ocean wanderings, pairs reunite and after a brief display begin mating. Soon each female lays her enormous white egg on the reddish clay among the lava stones. When the chicks hatch they are already large and plump, varying in color from chocolate brown to light cream. As no nest has been built, the young waddle uncertainly into the shady bushes while their parents fly off to feed, returning infrequently to present their little ones with a gulletful of rich oily fish. This routine will last for several months, until the young match the great size of the adults, gradually replacing their brown fluff with long, smooth feathers.

By November or December a new activity pervades the colony. In the late afternoon, as the air grows cool and damp in the lingering cold season, the pairs now launch into frequent sessions of frantic display. One by one the couples engage in a series of highly ritualized exercises, bill clapping, gaping, symbolic preening, sky-pointing—all in bursts of excitement that mount and die repeatedly. This behavior will continue, sometimes involving a third, stray, bird in a triangular formation, until the end of January when the last of the young, now totally developed and much resembling their parents, have walked to the south edge of the island and spread their great wings to sail off into the trade winds.

By February the heavy rains of the warm season arrive and the mockingbirds and Darwin's finches begin nesting in their turn. The pugnacious lava lizards, strangely colorful in this place, fight territorial battles, while their larger relatives, the male marine iguanas, reach the peak of their brilliant coloration as the females engage in stubborn disputes over the sparse dirt patches for nesting. When the seasonal plants have gone to seed, the Galápagos doves begin raising their own young beneath unobtrusive rock slabs, walking busily to and fro searching for food among the dry grasses. Along the wild sea cliffs and white sandy beaches sea lion families bark and cavort. The great seabirds, albatrosses and boobies, have temporarily left the island, but the life flow never stops.

The Galápagos World

Chapter Five

Lava and Life

A large variety of life forms thrives in great concentrations in many parts of the Galápagos Islands. Very often these forms are governed by the forces of volcanism that continue to reshape the archipelago. Just as when the islands were first being colonized by these organisms, plants and animals today continue to strive to invade the tormented volcanic cones and craters and the bleak expanses of fresh lavas that occasionally flow over the old land. Sometimes, after thousands of years, during which time a gradual succession of the living beings has established itself on the slowly degrading rocks, a sudden recurrence of volcanic activity may brusquely obliterate an entire wild community, leaving no trace of its existence. Then the process of colonization begins again, as simple life forms set out to gain a foothold on the unclaimed new land, and the area is progressively reclaimed by these plants and animals.

This process is perhaps best witnessed in Sullivan Bay and on the small island of Bartolomé. On climbing to its summit, barely one hundred meters above sea level, I have many times rediscovered the stupendous mineral view, a world of geology. At sunrise the calm orange-colored tuff sand beaches, the round, eroded cinder cones, the sharp pinnacle rock, all receive their first bath of golden light. Beyond a narrow stretch of sea the white sands on the shoreline of Santiago Island shine resplendent. Inland, a scan of the dark terrain reveals a land where time seems to have halted long ago. Like a frozen ocean, a black lava flow stretches flat and bleak, here and there surrounding cones and small mountains of tuff, or solidified ash, and red-tinged heaps of volcanic scoria.

To me this has always been a place to amble quietly, examining every detail of the "pahoehoe" or ropy lava under each footstep, spread like a black basaltic mantle over the land formed about eighty years ago. Now sunbaked and constantly swept by the salty sea breeze, it extends in endless swirls and folds, bubbles, ripples, spatters, and dribbles, all frozen in bluish-black glazed shapes. I always wonder what might have lived here before the lava annihilated it in a fiery blanket. Arid coastal vegetation probably dotted the land, as it still does on the adjacent older terrain missed by the flow. Here and there in the contorted shapes of the lava the intact molds of branches from small trees and bushes can be recognized where they left their imprint before burning away in the scorching matter. Yet not far away a small plant probes hesitantly out of a narrow fissure. Its copper-colored leaves are so thin that it is not obviously alive, but two or three minute starlike white flowers spread from the extremities of its fragile twigs. These tiny *Mollugo* plants are dispersed randomly on the bare lava, as well as some rare small clumps of the dwarfed *Brachycereus* cacti and sparse lichens. Here the timeless story of the fantastic struggle of all the Galápagos creatures, striving to colonize a new sterile land, is told. And when they have achieved a foothold, the volcanoes reawaken and once again disgorge their obliterating flows of lava. This cycle of colonization and destruction is repeated on countless occasions, yet each and every time the diverse life forms struggle into existence again.

In the interior of Santiago or James Island shredded, hazy clouds envelop the relatively low and ancient summit. Under this blanket of humidity a dense green forest grows, filled with ferns and other mist-loving plants. Here a small remnant of the island race of giant tortoises still lives. But many introduced animals also roam the hillsides, preying on the native fauna and devastating the vegetation. At the opposite end of the elongated island, the land descends quickly to James Bay. There the lava slopes are favored by abundant plant life, and tucked behind a mangrove-covered brown beach a tranquil saltwater lagoon offers shelter to a small flock of greater flamingos. About five hundred of these elegant birds inhabit the salt ponds of the archipelago. When the sun sinks low over the distant outline of the Isabela

Island volcanoes and its rays turn to red, the slender forms of the James Bay flamingos cast inflamed reflections on the dark surface of their mangrove pool. In the dry grassland, studded with silver-bark palo santo (*Bursera*) trees near the shore, beautiful Galápagos doves search for dried seeds after the brief rainy season, their camouflage brown color highlighted by bright pink feet and sky-blue eye-rings. Sometimes the endemic hawks swoop down and pluck them from the air as they explode into flight.

Farther down the coast the sea has dug intricate arched grottoes and tunnels in the lava. Galápagos fur seals play in the deep clear water, having made a comeback from near extinction caused by human exploitation at the turn of the century. The fur seals have dense, thick coats featuring two distinct layers of hair: a compact growth of stiff guard hairs and a warm underlayer of fine wool, which gives them effective protection against the cold water. Although the waters here are often quite cool, the equatorial sun is generally torrid and the fur seals seek out the rocky shores where they can find plenty of shady clefts and sleep in relative comfort. At the James Bay grottoes their strange screams and groans bellow from beneath rock slabs as they squabble for preferred positions. When the heat becomes overpowering near noontime they take frequent dips in the cooling water. Plunging gracefully head first from a meter or two above the surface, a seal's streamlined body enters the water in a long curve, leaving a thin trail of tiny air bubbles that escape from dry fur. Weaving its silvery way back to the surface, the seal will float for a few minutes, often dangling upside down, and then haul itself with amazing ease onto the steep, slippery rocks. The water drains rapidly from the fur, giving the seals a well-combed look. Snorting and puffing and threatening with their very sharp teeth, they lumber back to their favorite shady spots.

Even though the Galápagos fur seals have evolved into a subspecies, they, like other fur seals, are well adapted to the sub-Antarctic regions where they originated. They suffer in the heat and love the cold, rough seas. It is thus interesting to consider how they traveled, perhaps over thousands of years, up the cold coast of South America (where another form now exists) and out to the Galápagos Islands, following the cool waters of the Humboldt and South Equatorial currents.

The Sociable Sea Lions

Forming another integral part of the Galápagos world are the friendly and playful sea lions. Closely related to the California species, they live in many noisy colonies throughout the islands. One such happy concentration is found on the Plazas Islands, not far from Academy Bay. These are two small, elongated islands jutting into the sea off the eastern tip of Santa Cruz Island. There are no beaches on these islands, and so the sea lions—perhaps a thousand in number—laze on the slippery, sloping rocks that form the shore.

I vividly recall my first visit to this place. I had just turned ten when our small boat eased itself into the clear, sheltered waters between the two islands. We were immediately overwhelmed by the din that drifted to us with the wind. The monotonous, incessant barks of the old bulls mingled with plaintive cries from numerous mothers and pups calling to one another. A group of inquisitive adolescents detached itself from the coastline and swam out to investigate us. On the shore sleek youngsters leaped and chased one another in small tidepools among the glistening black rocks, while golden-furred cows dozed in the sun.

Sea lion society is carefully structured. Females select a spot along the shoreline to give birth, while large males will stake out individual territories, each one including as many females as possible. The males will eagerly defend their bit of shoreline against any intruding bulls, and even against sharks and humans. They will patrol their territory day and night, only occasionally taking trips to feed or short naps on the shore. Challengers are driven away furiously in long underwater pursuits, and sometimes there are vicious, bloody encounters. Most often, however, a dominant bull will maintain his position for a few days or perhaps a few weeks until, tired from the exertion, he will allow another male, stronger and fresher, to take over sovereignty. The half-mile coastline in South Plaza may be divided up at any one time by about a dozen bulls, each coveting a segment of shore and a group of females. The cows pup at any time of year, but most often during the cooler months. Birth is rapid for a sea lion, and the newborn soon begins calling to his mother, and she to him, in the most affectionate manner. She will assist the pup in his initial swim, carrying him by the nape to the water's edge and holding him in the shallows while he paddles about clumsily. He will develop quickly, doubling his birth weight by about two months of age, when he joins others of his size to frolic endlessly near the shore during his mother's long fishing trips. The adolescent pups devise countless tricks for amusement, nibbling at the dominant bull's flipper, porpoising through the water, somersaulting into the air, and even body surfing along the crests of waves rolling into shore. They are turbulent characters and display an unabatable urge to play. Anything can be used as a toy by these cavorting juveniles, be it a seashell, a branch, or a marine iguana returning from feeding. The object will be sunk, tossed, and pushed endlessly about, but somehow never damaged. When a boat drops its anchor between the two islands, the sea lions' curiosity is inevitably sparked. They will inspect and tug at the anchor chain, blow bubbles beneath the hull, and sometimes leap clear into the skiff for closer scrutiny. By the time the pup is eight months old he may begin fishing and fending for himself, but if his mother gives birth to a new baby, he may well regain her acceptance and continue suckling alongside his new brother or sister.

A sea lion's life is not always simple and beautiful. Many dangers lurk deep beneath the Pacific waters for the inexperienced young venturing out to sea. Hammerhead sharks or killer whales may eat them; I have seen horribly mutilated individuals return to die on the shore. Massive attacks by flies can infect the slightest scratch or cut and are the cause of many deaths among the small pups. Disease can take a high toll too: eye infections may render them blind, and a type of pox will paralyze and kill them.

Ochre-colored land iguanas also inhabit South Plaza. In the open terrain covered with the tender yellow portulaca blossoms that open in the late afternoon during the brief rains, and among the *Opuntia* cactus clumps, they meander, plucking flowers, fruits, and shoots off the arid vegetation. Finches flutter from one cactus blossom to another, absorbing the sweet nectar and unformed seeds. The humid oceanic wind rises along the tall south-facing cliff, and black and white Audubon shearwaters veer and swoop before entering their deep nesting cavities in the sheer lava face where swallow-tailed gulls sleep on the small ledges.

A Predator: The Galápagos Hawk

Fearlessness and inquisitiveness about humans are traits shared by many Galápagos animals. People did not appear in the islands until very recently, and therefore the wildlife have not undergone the lengthy learning process about human destruction so common elsewhere. Probably more important, there are almost no terrestrial predators native to Galápagos. Because the animals did not have to depend heavily on fear for their survival, their inherent curiosity has not been a disadvantage. While this curiosity is clearly visible in the sea lions, it is displayed even more obviously by the Galápagos hawk, the only diurnal raptor.

When I was a child and we traveled among the islands we often encountered these hawks near the beaches where we landed—or rather they encountered us. Usually we saw the immature birds, speckled brown in color (the all-black adults, which had probably satisfied their curiosity about humans at an earlier stage of their life, were less often seen). These young birds would follow us about insistently, their curiosity unquenchable. Sometimes as many as thirty or forty would perch around our campsite, cocking their heads in apparent astonishment. A large group would follow us as we hiked, hovering one meter above our heads if the wind permitted. Once, when surrounded by inquisitive hawks, I felt that irrepressible human impulse to reach out and touch their sharp, shiny talons, and they accepted the gesture with more curiosity than fear.

Unfortunately, their tameness has not always served the hawks well. Populations on islands now inhabited by humans were slaughtered because they killed chickens, or for the simple reason that they were unafraid.

Though the hawks are found in all parts of the islands, they usually nest in the arid coastal areas. Each pair holds a year-round territory in which they build two or three nests on rocky outcroppings or in large trees. These they may use interchangeably from year to year, adding one more layer of nesting material each time. When they are protecting eggs or chicks, usually during July, August, or September, the gentle, inquisitive birds turn into furies, screaming and diving repeatedly and hitting with closed talons if approached. Sad to say, this behavior has incited slaughter of the hawks by those humans who cannot tolerate being intimidated by an animal.

One interesting trait of the Galápagos hawks is that sometimes they are polyandric, that is, two or even three males may be mated to a single female. They will all defend the territory, care for the nest, and feed the young equally, staying together year after year. The Galápagos hawks are endemic to the islands, having evolved differently from every other type of hawk in the world. Exquisitely adapted to the arid conditions of the Galápagos coastal areas, they feed on anything from grasshoppers and caterpillars to birds, centipedes, marine iguanas, small lava lizards, and sea lion placentae.

Because of their excellent adaptation the hawks inhabit all the extremes of the Galápagos environment. In the moist greenery of Alcedo Crater on Isabela I have watched them use the gentle, grazing tortoises as convenient perches, and on the spacious rim of the volcano of Fernandina they have followed me for hours, intrigued, all the while soaring, playing, and squabbling acrobatically in the wind. Along Fernandina's rugged coast, where even the smallest plant often seems out of place, the hawks always seem to be present. Here they rely chiefly on the marine iguanas for their survival. It is strange to watch a raptor sitting in the midst of a group of these iguanas who show no fear, but appear simply to trust in their numbers for protection. For a long time the hawk may study them intently, then single out a victim and suddenly pounce. Unless the reptile can manage to take refuge under a rock slab, it makes an easy prey, although it is too heavy for the hawk to lift in flight until it is partially consumed. At Cape Douglas on Fernandina I spotted a sharp rock outcropping where the resident pair of hawks had the habit of taking their meals. The well-cleaned carcasses strewn on the ground attested to the birds' dependence on these strange marine lizards for their food.

A Society of Lava Lizards

The little lava lizards are common everywhere on the Galápagos. These terrestrial reptiles vary considerably from one island to another, showing many differences in shape, size, and color. Seven species exist within the archipelago; one is distributed on several central islands, while the others have evolved separately in the isolation of their own islands. Some, such as the lava lizards on Pinzon, have extensive rusty and orange patches covering their sleek bodies, while others are almost completely black. The type on Hood Island is nearly twice as large as the others. All, however, share a strong territorial instinct, and every yard of suitable habitat on nearly every island supports its own little pugnacious owner. Except on the humid highlands and a few lifeless, sunbaked lava flows, this inconspicuous reptilian society thrives with the most bewildering success. The lava lizards prosper in the midst of seabird colonies, and can also be seen basking on the heaving stomachs of sleeping sea lions or using the heads of immobile marine iguanas as a lookout perch for flies. Along the coast where life is sparse they may turn to small crabs and other little intertidal invertebrates for food, and during the seasonal rains their diets are supplemented with petals and small flowers. When the opportunity arises, they relish scorpions, large juicy cockroaches, and centipedes more than half their own size.

Competition for living space is constant and intense, and both males and females must continuously fend off intruders of their respective sex. Fights are both ritualized and effective. The two opponents will line up in a head-to-tail position, with colorful throats inflated and heads bobbing aggressively. They move together in cautious jerks, slapping each other repeatedly with powerful swats of their tails. If this ritual fails to decide the outcome, they may end up in a very unritualized tussle that sometimes results in a snapped-off tail. The appendage will grow back in due time, and the boneless, cartilaginous substitute will prove as useful as the original.

Tiny hatchling lizards lead precarious lives. They own no territories and must constantly be on the lookout lest they be devoured by large aggressive males. This cannibalism may serve to maintain a stable population when hatching success is very high. Spiders and centipedes, which are eaten by the adult lizard, may also prey on the small young, and lava herons and mockingbirds are still another threat.

Death of a Shearwater

Chapter Six

The Will to Survive

The first time I visited Tower Island, after my initial enchantment at discovering the nesting frigates and red-footed boobies, I wandered farther inland and then along the coast. Among the dwarfed, leafless forest of silvery *Bursera* trees I saw more frigates and more boobies, all busily going about their duties of protecting and rearing their precious offspring. Later I sat alone on the edge of a low cliff for a long time. Waves were washing in and out, the wind was warm and humid over the water. Where the current that skirted the shore veered off the rocks and for a moment bucked the movement of the waves, I saw something small and black bobbing along the crests. It was a shearwater floating, immobile, drenched to the skin. His feathers had somehow lost their waterproofing and now he was waterlogged, unable to move or fly. A few brown fishes rose from beneath and inspected him, and a slow school of large sharks drifted silently by, following the shore. Cold and half sinking, he was doomed, yet he shook his head to rid himself of the water as if to take off once more.

As a human I found this imminent prospect of death inadmissible. I wanted to dive, swim, warm him, save him. The sharks returned, leisurely cruising the shoreline, causing my own survival instinct to awaken, and I compared my position to that of the drowning bird. I realized that I was only another warm-blooded vertebrate, one of many in a world where only the agile and intelligent survive. Great frigate birds were flying by, searching for food, and a few immature red-footed boobies were learning hesitantly to dive from the air after some invisible little fishes beneath the surface. All were going about their own lives intensely, trying to preserve and prolong it as best they could.

By the time I returned to the little beach where I had landed I somehow understood the death of the shearwater, and I began to accept it. Death has a place in the harmony of life.

By the entrance of the bay tropic birds were coming in, circling and screaming powerfully in their courtship flight, their energy filling the air over the water and before the towering cliffs. In the bushes near the beach sat white-headed juvenile frigates, almost the size of the adults. With sudden decision, some would spread their great wings and lift lightly into the air. A few would circle and return; others would venture farther, attempting to pick some food off the water, but managing only to catch a floating twig. Occasionally one of them chased a booby or tropic bird to try and steal its catch of fish, but they did not succeed at this either. Late in the afternoon when the air grew cool I could see the same young frigates sitting each on its own perch, where the nests had long crumbled away. They were scanning the sky, anxiously waiting for their parents to return and feed them once more. Many were a year old already, yet they still needed parental help while they were sharpening their own skills. But soon their parents would leave and not return. Some would learn how to survive, but others would search for food in vain. After several weeks these would weaken, unable to fly any longer, and eventually return one last time to their weathered nest to starve in silence.

Next year the adults will breed again and produce another batch of young, and again only a few will succeed. For them to live, others of their race must die, for even in the vast ocean there is no room for increase. The essence of life is death, by predation or by replacement. It is a never-ending rotation and this is what keeps each species attuned to its environment.

To Eat and Be Eaten

On another island, at another time, I saw a large grasshopper feeding on the tender bud of a salty plant. As he consumed the nourishing stem I could see his brilliant colors reflecting the sunlight. On this shore he had started his life, huddling in the grassy patches as a big-headed, stubby larva. If he had spread his large wings in a sudden burst, I might have seen the delicate translucent membranes with their fine golden veins unfold like fans, but instead he stayed and continued to gnaw at the juicy plant. Suddenly a movement caught my eye as a male lava lizard approached, making precise bounds from rock to rock. He stalked briefly, then gave one last lurch and suddenly it was too late; the grasshopper was now held between firm reptilian jaws. In a few minutes he was dismantled and eaten, and no trace of him was left but a scar he had made on the salty plant. The satiated lizard flattened his body on a warm rock and began to doze. His small overlapping scales ran down his back in perfect lines. Each tiny triangle had a different color; some were bright red, yellow, light green, black, or white, but from a distance the lizard appeared gray. He would probably have no need to eat for several days. Although only a few inches long, he was a predator. Yet even he was not safe.

In the dry grass another reptile was moving slowly, silently, stopping and inspecting his surroundings as he advanced. A three-foot-long snake was gliding ever so cautiously between the parched, crumpled grass blades. Suddenly he came upon the lava lizard overlooking his territory, and he froze. His tail trembled slightly, and the lizard, intrigued, hopped closer. Perhaps the unwary lizard thought he had seen the motion of an insect under a dry leaf; in any case he was not prepared when the snake struck. After throwing a few constricting coils around the lizard, the snake began to swallow it head first, and the struggle was soon over. In a few minutes the lizard had disappeared, having simply become a swelling in a snake's body.

This I witnessed on a calm, hot afternoon. It had been a different lizard on yet another island, but I had nonetheless been able to observe a complete episode in the flow of life. Before my eyes life was flowing from one organism to another. Like the shearwater, the grasshopper and lizard had to die for others to live, thus perpetuating life in an endless succession.

Righting the Wrongs

It took an uncountable number of years for the Galápagos creatures to become so well adjusted to their volcanic home. Then, with man came trouble for these gentle animals. The tortoise and fur seal populations were drastically reduced, and many other animals suffered also, although less conspicuously. Mice, rats, cats, dogs, pigs, goats, donkeys, horses, and cows disembarked from the ships that visited the islands and, together with a considerable sprinkling of invertebrates and plants such as fire ants, earthworms and quinine trees, began invading and gravely affecting many of the insular ecosystems.

It is difficult to imagine the Galápagos before man arrived. Even though there is a great wealth of wildlife and nature to wonder at today, there have been many subtle destructions and there are but a few places that are still pristine. Perhaps as many as seventy-five thousand tortoises lived on the islands at one time; now a maximum of ten thousand remain. Of fourteen island subspecies described by early scientists, only ten remain as viable populations, and many of these are threatened by a variety of introduced mammals.

By the middle of the twentieth century concern for the unique ecosystem of the Galápagos and the plight of its rare inhabitants began to grow among scientists and conservationists. In 1959 an international organization, the Charles Darwin Foundation, was set up to coordinate efforts to protect the islands. That year was the hundredth anniversary of the publication of Charles Darwin's theory of evolution, and the government of Ecuador made all uninhabited areas in the islands (about 88 percent of the total land surface) its first national park. By this time most of the direct killing of the native animals had ended, as it was no longer an integral part of life for the people living on the islands. But the feral mammals introduced by early sailors on almost all the islands represented a more complex problem. In many places goats, donkeys, horses, or cattle had stripped the vegetation and sometimes trampled the tortoise nests. Some of the islands had dogs and pigs, and almost all had feral house cats, and these carnivores attacked and destroyed some tortoise populations. Land iguanas were exterminated on certain islands and dark-rumped petrels nesting in the humid forests suffered greatly. The introduced rats caused tremendous damage, eating the eggs and young of the tortoises and other defenseless animals; they caused the extermination on most islands of the endemic rice rats, the only native Galápagos land mammal besides the Galápagos bats.

In the early 1960s efforts were made to slow or reverse this man-induced destruction. Financed by UNESCO, the Charles Darwin Research Station was set up in Academy Bay to assess priorities and begin the work of conservation. In the years that followed, the National Park Administration was organized and began working actively on many aspects of the islands' conservation. Together the two establishments have accomplished a number of very important goals. Park wardens have exterminated wild goats on several medium-sized islands and are approaching total success on some of the larger ones. The Galápagos National Park Administration has embarked on many large-scale projects—among them monitoring tortoise populations throughout the islands, controlling tourism through strict regulations, and eradicating several introduced plants and animals. In cooperation with the Darwin Station, it is breeding the most endangered races of tortoises and land iguanas in captivity in order to repopulate their home islands.

On Hood Island the most distinct form of saddleback tortoises once existed, but when the breeding programs were initiated, only fifteen individuals remained, three of them males. All were taken into captivity to reproduce in open-air pens, as in the wild they had been too dispersed to meet for mating. During the years that followed, the goats on the island were exterminated by intensive hunting. So far several dozen young tortoises bred in captivity have been set free—thus the original balance of this island's ecosystem is well on its way to being fully restored.

This is one outstandingly successful episode in the fight to save the giant tortoise, but on other islands the story has been a sadder one. On Pinzon Island black rats have been eating tortoise hatchlings for years. Raised to an age where they are no longer vulnerable, many young have been returned, but there appears to be no way of ridding the island of rats. From Pinta Island only one male giant tortoise has been brought to the breeding pens, and despite years of search no female has been found to join him; he may be the last of his race.

Preserving the Galápagos ecosystem and restoring its natural balance will take many more years, if the problems don't prove insurmountable. Unfortunately Ecuador is not a rich country and can only set aside limited finances for its island national park. Most of the necessary work consumes a tremendous amount of time, energy, and money. For many years the Darwin Station has been funneling private donations into this effort, for which it appeals internationally. But still, funding always falls short and many urgent projects cannot be begun.

Perhaps these efforts to heal the human-inflicted damage are too late, as in the case of Floreana Island where the gentle giant tortoises will never again be seen. But all of us engaged in the work of conservation believe that someday most of the islands will be restored to their delicate equilibrium and we will again see the untroubled, harmonious scenes that make the Galápagos world so fascinating.

A Lost Dream

Galápagos will always mean to me a vast freedom, a place where total wildness, animals and plants, mountains and ocean, existed unmarred by human progress and modernization. But in the last two or three years it has become clear that this wild freedom belongs to the past.

To cope with the flow of tourists and safeguard the islands' fragile nature, the Galápagos National Park Administration has had to set up a system of marked trails that visitors must respect. Many beaches that used to be marked only by sea lion and pelican tracks are now the landing place for cruise ships. The tourist boom with its promise of sudden wealth has changed some of our neighbors from relaxed residents to aggressive businessmen. Intrigue and jealousy have permeated dealings on the islands. A forty-kilometer road has been built across Santa Cruz Island to serve the thirty or forty cars that have replaced the traditional horses, mules, and donkeys. Two fatal crashes have already taken place. A few years ago everyone in our neighborhood rowed their skiffs to the village to do their errands; now my family is the only one that does not zoom across the bay with a powerful outboard motor.

It seems that we who feel no urge to change to the motorized system are clinging to a bygone era, a time when giant cacti were still allowed to grow in some village plots, when the oysters clung to the rocks at low tide, before the recurrent diesel fuel spills killed them.

Our closest neighbor, a German, has built a hotel near the beach where we swam and played as children. The lagoon where we used to watch fiddler crabs and seabirds has been fitted with dikes, locks, and an electric pump because the owner feels that it is more attractive to maintain the pond in front of his hotel at full level all the time. The tides are allowed to rise and fall only under the supervision of hotel employees. Every morning a group of tourists boards a boat for a day's visit to some nearby island. As even the closest of these are a few hours distant, the tourists get to see the land only during the midday hours, inevitably missing the subtle beauty of the sunrise, the early-morning courtship of the blue-footed boobies, or the late-afternoon activity at a sea lion colony.

I used to guide small groups of people on chartered motor sailing boats that carried between six and ten passengers. The trips lasted a leisurely two to three weeks and took in several of the more beautiful places in Galápagos, as opposed to the three- and four-day shifts now offered by the hotel and other large tours. We were a close-knit group in the confinement of these small boats, and I drew great pleasure from sharing my secrets and excitements with these enthusiastic people. Now the trend in tourism is toward large groups of sixty or more and much shorter stays. Many visitors arrive with gross misconceptions about the islands, some even expecting to find gorillas and elephants.

The increasing number of tourists (fourteen thousand in 1978) has forced the Galápagos National Park Administration to establish strict rules to prevent alterations to the wildlife and plants of the islands. I often long for the time when the islands were so isolated and little known that there was no need to set human controls. Yet it is comforting to know that the Galápagos Islands with their fantastic package of wild inhabitants, their wealth of aesthetic riches and unique scientific values, are being well taken care of, if taken care of they must be. The Galápagos National Park is one of the strictest and best managed in South America and through the administration's efforts some of man's severe wrongdoings have been erased. Several of the islands have been restored to their condition of more than a century ago. At least the flow of tourism will keep away large-scale fisheries and other disastrous exploitations. If I feel a little sad that the primitive freedom of the Galápagos has been lost, I am gratified that the islands themselves have at last received the respect that they deserve.

Last Struggle

When I was a child we would hunt green turtles that entered the mangrove-sheltered bay not far from our home. They would come into the quiet cove at night during the warm season and occasionally we would decide to catch one to vary the taste of wild goat meat, lobster, and fish. At dusk when the tide was high we would glide our rowboat silently through the calm water, waiting intently. I might be rowing while my father stood at the bow, scanning the surface in the dimming light, holding a long bamboo rod rigged with a big shark hook straight before him. In the dark shadows along the drooping mangrove foliage a muffled breath could be heard momentarily and I would angle the skiff and row cautiously toward the place. My father would now be leaning forward, his pole extended. Then he would plunge the hook deep into the water and, if he was lucky, snag the escaping turtle near the bottom. A flurry of splashes would follow as we pulled the animal closer, and we had to be careful not to upset the small boat. The turtle would break the surface repeatedly, breathing frantically in her desperate struggle to flee. But we would grab her flipper, hoist her on board, and slide her on her back onto the wooden floor. After a successful catch, we would have an abundance of delicious meat for several days.

This was ten or fifteen years ago, when everyone in Academy Bay caught turtles from time to time. We did not know much about conservation and were not aware that sea turtles all over the world were diminishing because of man's abuse. More important, we really did not think of the turtles as individuals with lives to lead and problems to face. In essence, we were predators and they were the prey.

Then a few things changed around us. Turtles were less frequently seen along the mangrove fringe, and beef became available. As a result we did not eat any turtle meat for several years. One evening about five years ago we were watching the blue lights of phosphorescence play among the dangling roots of the mangroves. We noticed that there were many turtles gliding about in luminous halos, and a sudden urge took us to go out and catch one again, as in days past. Once again I coasted the skiff toward the quiet breath in the dark, and as before, my father was ready with his long rod and hook. But this time I did not hear the breath of a prey ready to be caught, but rather the breathing of a gentle animal living silently through the ages. When the sharp hook pierced the leathery skin at the base of her flipper and she flailed and splashed as we hoisted her into the boat, I no longer felt as if I were witnessing a successful catch; instead I was seeing an innocent life in the grasp of a deadly power. She gave a final struggle, a last hopeless effort toward freedom and life, but we prevailed, and I began to feel sick at heart. We carried through on our macabre mission, for we were in need of protein and we had set out to fulfill this need. But the following day the meat tasted far less delicious than it once had, and I swore that as long as I lived I would not kill another green turtle. In those few years I had come to learn something about life, and I now understood that there was no other place for a free-living turtle than in the dark swaying seaweed pastures nourished by the mighty ocean currents. She belonged there, or on some remote beach unblemished by human footprints, where she would haul herself onto the sand to lay her eggs, perpetuating her kind. Even if by some mishap she was caught in the crushing jaws of a killer whale—she belonged there rather than in the bottomless basket of a human being.

A Life of Learning

Thanks to my Galápagos home I have had a special perspective on life and the natural world, something that many members of my race may never even glimpse. I have learned to look, and I have learned to see and sometimes to understand. I have seen the hidden meanings in the determined travels of a giant tortoise, the territoriality of a male lava lizard, the eagerness of a frigate bird fiercely robbing a terrified booby. The tortoise is not stupid to pursue what appears to be an aimless path; instead she is searching for adequate conditions in which to lay her eggs. The lava lizard is not selfish because he defends his territory against other males; rather he is protecting an area where he will find the food he needs and attract females to reproduce. And frigates are not wicked for harassing other birds, but are only responding to the urgent necessity of feeding their young; pilfering that extra bit may mean the difference between life and death for them. Within the urge of the tortoise, the aggressiveness of the lizard, and the insistence of the robbing frigate is hidden the unflinching desire to pass on a precious package of genetic messages to the forthcoming generation, sending with it any slight improvement in the quality of life to the future of each race. One could say that all these interrelating forms on earth are in a fierce and unrelenting competition, an eternal deadlock, each trying mercilessly to usurp life from the other. Yet this is the projection of a human whose knowledge is hampered by too little perspective and not enough detail. Even within the apparent harshness of the natural world lies a fundamental harmony. Every member of this living network depends on his fellows for his healthy survival, perhaps as much as on the air he breathes.

Trying to understand is perhaps one of humanity's most inherent traits, be it to understand the growth of a grass blade, the symbiosis of lichens, the purpose of an ant, or the origin of the Milky Way. Constantly we try to comprehend, and we find answers, so many answers. Sometimes they are grotesque in their simplicity. Certainly, the quest for answers is a most exciting one, and the answers themselves may bring us even greater satisfaction. But then sometimes another question comes to my mind: Why do we expect to find an explanation to everything around us?

Above my table is a large spider living behind one of the roof beams. I love spiders, particularly this one, velvety gray and brown. I have watched him for a long time; every evening he comes out, and if he is successful, he catches a moth flittering in the light. But what does he know of his surroundings? He lives behind that beam that was brought here from a continent great distances away. In fact, his own ancestors probably came from the same place, but he doesn't know that. He lives in this house, but does not understand why it is here and what function it serves. To him the lights go on and off and sometimes the air is filled with the vibrations of music. Now, we fully accept that he does not comprehend how his world came about, and what is happening to it, or if anything might take place before life begins or after it ends. Why, then, can't we accept those problems that are too great for our own minds to solve?

A New Adventure

Three years ago I met a young man who was working with the Galápagos National Park Administration. His name was Alan and I knew from our first meeting that he was someone very special. He came from the United States on a United Nations mission sent to help implement the Galápagos National Park master plan. A little more than a year later we were married, without great to-do, in the city of Quito. It seems to me particularly fitting that I should have met my husband while he was working for the preservation of the Galápagos wilderness, and I consider myself a very lucky person to be his wife. Together we have made many trips among the islands, exploring, sharing feelings and experiences, photographing nature and breathing its freedom. We have swum off a mile-long beach we had all to ourselves, and have awakened to the bustling, bird-filled dawn of Tower Island. There have been some unpleasant times too, for the Galápagos environment is not conducive to carefree amusement. There were nights we spent vainly trying to keep dense swarms of mosquitoes out of our tent, and I remember occasions when we stayed out too late and had to feel our way home in pitch darkness among thick thorny scrub and jagged lava.

Together we built ourselves a home in Academy Bay. It is made of lava blocks and wood, with a large indoor garden. All year round the wind blows through its large, screened windows; the ocean is always visible in front, and the rising sun shines into our bed on bright days. The national park boundary runs a few meters from our back door, and the dry giant cactus forest grows untouched all around us. A female lava lizard has staked out her territory inside the house, making short trips to the outside world but always returning to the safety of our living room. In the late afternoon our front door is besieged by Darwin's finches waiting for a cookie handout.

Even so, we have become hungry for a new adventure. The volcanoes are still wild and beautiful, and the animals are as intriguing as ever, but with some regret I realize that we must move on to accomplish our work and our goals. We do not wish to spend a lifetime brushing against these people of Academy Bay, who are so different from us in their eager striving for progress. People like them exist everywhere, but there are also others, who are no longer found in Galápagos, those whose values are not dominated by profit. Therefore I shall have to retract my roots someday soon, as Alan did when he left his native Massachusetts, so that we may wander without any real commitment for a while, exploring some of nature's other wonders before settling down to raise a family.

A part of me will remain behind on these rugged islands, but I will also take with me something infinitely precious that I have acquired from them: the capacity to learn through my senses, to understand some of nature's secrets through my feelings, rather than through science and scholarly teachings alone.

Selected Bibliography

Not included are numerous scientific papers on practically all aspects of Galápagos natural history.

Black, J. *Galápagos, Archipelago del Ecuador.* Quito: Impremita Europa (Charles Darwin Foundation and World Wild Life Fund), 1973.

Bowman, R. I. *The Galápagos.* Proceeding Symposia of the Galápagos International Scientific Project. Los Angeles: University of California Press, 1966.

* Brower, K., and Porter, E. *Galápagos: The Flow of Wildness.* 2 vols. New York: Sierra Club and Ballantine Books, 1968.

Carlquist, S. *Island Life.* Garden City, N.Y.: Natural History Press, 1965.

Darwin, Charles. *The Voyage of the Beagle.* Garden City, N.Y.: Doubleday, 1962.

* Eibl-Eibesfeldt, I. *Galápagos: Noah's Ark of the Pacific.* Garden City, N.Y.: Doubleday, 1961.

Eibl-Eibesfeldt, I. *Galápagos: Die Arche Noah Im Pazfik.* Munich: R. Piper Verlag, 1977.

Harris, M. P. *A Field Guide to the Birds of Galápagos.* London: Collins; New York: Taplinger, 1974.

Lack, D. *Darwin's Finches: An Essay on the General Biological Theory of Evolution.* Gloucester, Mass.: Peter Smith, 1968.

McBirney, A. R., and Williams, H. *Geology and Petrology of the Galápagos Islands.* Washington, D.C.: Geological Society of America, 1969.

* Nelson, J. B. *Galápagos: Islands of Birds.* London: Longmans Green; New York: Morrow, 1968.

† Nordlie, B. E. "Morphology and Structure of the Western Galápagos Volcanoes and a Model for Their Origin." *Geological Society of America Bulletin* 84: 2931–2956.

Perry, R. *The Galápagos Islands.* New York: Dodd, Mead, 1972.

† Simkin, T., and Howard, K. A. "Caldera Collapse in the Galápagos Islands." *Science* 169: 429–437.

Slevin, J. R. *The Galápagos Islands: A History of Their Exploration.* Occasional Papers of the California Academy of Sciences, No. 25, 1959.

Thornton, I. *Darwin's Islands: A Natural History of the Galápagos.* Garden City, N.Y.: Natural History Press, 1971.

Wiggins, I. L., and Porter, D. M. *Flora of the Galápagos Islands.* Stanford, Cal.: Stanford University Press, 1971.

* Out of print.
† Reprints from cited papers.

Galápagos Natural History

Appendix I

Origin of the Islands

Geographical Setting and Surrounding Bathymetry

The Galápagos Islands, consisting of thirteen to fifteen major islands and many more small ones, lie athwart the equator some one thousand kilometers west of South America. They rise from a shallow submarine plateau, the Galápagos Platform, which ranges from 350 to 900 meters in depth, and averages 1800 meters above the surrounding ocean floor. The northern islands in the group—Wenman, Culpepper, Pinta, Marchena, and Tower—are separated from this plateau, and because their base is at a greater depth than that of the southern islands, their structures are much larger than they appear. Starting near the northern end of the archipelago and extending all the way to Costa Rica is a prominent submarine ridge, the Cocos Ridge, whose depth averages less than 2200 meters. Toward the east is the Carnegie Ridge, with an average depth of 2500 meters; it reaches toward South America, but is terminated by the Peruvian Trench. One thousand kilometers to the west of the island group runs the crest of the East Pacific Rise, a lengthy spreading ridge where most of the tectonic plates making up the Pacific Ocean floor originate. The Galápagos Islands ride on the Nazca Plate, which is drifting toward, and being subducted beneath, the South American continent.

Oceanic Volcanoes and Hot Spots

It is generally accepted that the Galápagos are of strictly oceanic origin, that is, they were never connected by dry land to any continental mass. At one time the presence of diverse life forms on the islands gave rise to several theories supporting the former existence of a partial or complete land bridge with Central or South America, which later subsided into the sea. These theories have been discredited in recent years for lack of geological support.

The Galápagos are identified geologically as one of the earth's so-called hot spots, centers of acutely hot magma rising from deep within the mantle of the earth and producing intense volcanic activity on the surface. A number of such points have been recognized all over the world, the Hawaiian Islands being perhaps the best documented and in many ways the most similar to the Galápagos. Because the tectonic plates of the earth's crust drift slowly over such hot spots, there is a tendency to produce volcanoes of progressive age as they move gradually away from the center of activity. The Nazca Plate, on which the Galápagos rest, has over millions of years been drifting toward South America. As a result, the islands closest to that continent tend to be the oldest.

Age and Growth of the Islands

There remain a number of intriguing questions about the islands' origins. Which island appeared first? Is it one of the present islands in the group, or did the first island sink back into the sea? Did several islands rise simultaneously? Did any of these join to form one larger island? Or did an original land mass split up into various islands by subsidence and downfaulting?

The age of the islands is also uncertain. Accurate radiometric rock datings are made difficult by the small amount of initial radioactive material in Galápagos rocks and by the fact that most of the older terrains have been covered by more youthful lavas. Therefore there are few reliable dates that can be used in trying to establish when this volcanic process began, and when it might have been sufficiently advanced to pierce the surface of the sea and form the new Galápagos Islands. However, the patient work of several geologists long involved in unraveling these secrets has established with a fair degree of certainty that the present above-water volcanoes began appearing at least three million years ago.

Geology of the Islands

Volcanic Eruptions

The Galápagos constitute one of the most active set of oceanic volcanoes in the world, particularly the two large westerly islands, Isabela and Fernandina. Their large shield volcanoes exhibit frequent bursts of activity, usually as short-lived eruptions along fractures on their rim and flanks or within their enormous calderas. Large numbers of these eruptions have occurred during the short span of historic time, and many of these show very clearly the process of steady growth of the islands as each of the lava flows contributes more material to the bulk of land, often extending the shoreline some distance into the sea.

The seven volcanoes of Isabela and Fernandina islands are the youngest and by far the most active of the group. They are characterized by their large sizes, symmetrical shapes, and enormous central calderas. Frequent eruptions have been recorded during the short span of human history in the Galápagos, and numerous small eruptions have certainly gone unnoticed because of their short duration and the irregularity with which people have traveled among the islands. Although flank eruptions are common, much of the activity also takes place inside the large calderas and is thus even less likely to be observed. A caldera is formed when the magma withdraws from the volcano's subsurface chamber or is expelled by a large eruption.

When this supporting magma is removed, the overlying roof of the chamber collapses, creating an outsized crater, the caldera. This is precisely what occurred on Fernandina in 1968. Following a short period of violent explosive activity, the caldera increased in depth by 350 meters over a matter of a couple of weeks. In the decade since then volcanologists from the United States, and particularly Dr. Tom Simkin from the Smithsonian Institution, have made major advances in understanding the mechanisms of this extraordinary volcano. As a result this caldera collapse, a rarely witnessed phenomenon, has become the most thoroughly investigated to date.

The remaining islands, with perhaps the exception of some of the southeastern ones, have all had long periods of intense activity. These are dormant at present, although Santiago erupted as late as the nineteenth century, and it is almost certain that other recent eruptions have simply gone unobserved.

Uplift and Faulting

The islands of Hood, Barrington, Baltra, Seymour, Plazas, and the northeastern section of Santa Cruz appear to be mainly the result of upheaval of the ocean floor. They show few signs of above-water activity and consist largely of buckled and rifted portions of submarine lava flows that have been lifted out of the sea. Cliffs on these islands may show stratified layers of marine limestone containing invertebrate fossils between many lava flows, which probably issued either from undersea vents or from neighboring active islands.

Physical Setting of the Islands

Ocean Currents and Climate

The Galápagos repose at the confluence of two distinct systems of ocean currents, which accounts for their unique environment as well as for much of their diverse fauna. Although the islands are crossed by the equator, the waters around them give them a cool subtropical climate.

For six months out of the year, from about June to December, the islands are bathed in the cool waters of the South Equatorial Current. This season is referred to as the cool or "garua" season, from the Spanish word for drizzle. The South Equatorial Current is a combination of the Peru Oceanic Current, which flows up over great distances from the southern latitudes, and the Peru Coastal, or Humboldt, Current, which upwells along South America. These waters are pushed through the Galápagos in the garua season by the steady southeast trade winds. During this half of the year a rather unusual meteorological condition prevails. The air mass is cooled where it comes into contact with the cold waters, becoming bottom heavy, which suppresses normal vertical convection and thus thwarts condensation into rain. Instead, a well-defined inversion layer is created where the cool, humidity-laden lower layer of air meets the warm, dry one above. Misty clouds form at this level, precipitating almost exclusively in the form of drizzle and fog drip where the clouds come into contact with the mass of the island. As a result, most of the land areas both above and below this inversion layer are quite arid.

The second major flow of water affecting the islands is the much warmer and less saline El

Niño, which moves out of the Gulf of Panama from December to May. These waters flow south when the trade winds slacken, causing the South Equatorial Current to lose its force during this season. With the warm weather come heavy rains and thunderstorms, although weather conditions can be extremely variable; some years El Niño travels as far south as Peru, while in others it never reaches the Galápagos. This time of year, from January to May, is called the warm or rainy season.

A third important feature in the Galápagos waters is the Cromwell Current or Equatorial Undercurrent, a cold subsurface current that upwells where it encounters the western edge of the Galápagos Platform. It is responsible for the cool temperatures and rich marine life around Fernandina Island and the western coast of Isabela.

Arrival of Life

Means of Transport

Plants and animals can cross a vast stretch of ocean to become colonizers of such remote islands as the Galápagos in a variety of ways. Marine mammals as well as marine reptiles and many birds can easily span the distance by flying or swimming. Seawater flotation can bring a variety of plants and seeds, especially coastal and seawater forms, and winds can carry lightweight seeds and spores as well as small insects. Snails and certain seeds can be brought by migrating birds. However, the most important means of dispersal for both animals and plants is almost certainly the rafts of tangled vegetation disgorged from flooded continental rivers along the South American coast.

The selection of plant and animal types found in the Galápagos Islands today is a direct reflection of their capability to accomplish and survive such long travels. Thus birds are numerous whereas amphibians are absent, because they were unable to withstand prolonged contact with saltwater. Reptiles, which can easily live without food or fresh water for weeks because of their slow metabolism, are much more common than land mammals, which could not survive such privation.

Natural Selection

Whenever a plant or animal becomes established in a new environment, it is almost always poorly suited to function in that habitat. As a result, any individual harboring a trait somehow favorable to its survival will reproduce more successfully and pass on the advantage genetically to its offspring. If the founder population is small, this new quality will become dominant rather than be genetically flooded out. This factor was obviously very important for many of the Galápagos species.

Island Ecosystem

There is a series of niches in the Galápagos ecosystem that would be occupied by highly specialized organisms in similar continental ecosystems. Because it has been impossible for some of these forms to reach the islands and become established, the niches have remained vacant. Through evolution, however, unlikely forms have occasionally adapted to fill these niches, making use of the otherwise unexploited resources. Two classic examples are the woodpecker finch, which has taken the place of the absent woodpeckers, and the *Scalesia* tree, which has evolved from a group of plants that does not normally grow woody trunks into a forest-forming tree ten or twelve meters high where few other trees are present.

Another unusual aspect of the Galápagos ecosystem is its relative simplicity, for it comprises far fewer species of plants and animals than a comparatively diverse area on a large continent. Therefore the island ecosystem is very vulnerable to any change or further input. Because certain members of a more complete ecosystem have been absent (such as large predators), Galápagos wildlife are adaptively unprepared for and defenseless against them.

Vegetation Zones

All the islands exceeding six hundred meters in altitude show at least two vegetational zones: the dry coastal belt, which turns green only in response to the heavy downpours of the warm season (January–May), and a highland green zone, which receives enough fog and drizzle in all seasons to remain green, and often quite luxuriant, all year round. Santa Cruz, being one of the older islands and having fairly high elevations, shows the best pattern of vegetation zoning in the entire group. On its south slope, which is best exposed to wind and rain, these areas of plant growth have been divided into seven distinct zones: (1) the littoral zone, where salt plants such as mangroves, *Sesuvium, Batis, Nolana,* and *Scaevola* are found; (2) the arid coastal zone, consisting of xerophytic plants such as cacti, *Bursera, Maythenus, Croton, Cordia,* and many others, particularly shrubs; (3) the transitional zone, where species from the wet and dry areas mix and a number of specific types such as *Erythrina, Pisonia, Piscidia,* and *Waltheria* are found; (4) the green, or *Scalesia,* zone, which is lushest and has the highest canopy, consisting mostly of *Scalesia pedunculata,* but also of *Psidium, Zanthoxilum, Tournefortia,* epiphytes like *Tillandsia* and *Peperomia,* and many vines; (5) the brown zone, which gets its name from the thick fronds of liverworts that thrive in this foggy region and cover the abundant *Psidium* trees (this zone has been almost entirely destroyed by agriculture); (6) the miconia belt, which is the wettest area on the island, receiving more than two meters of rain a year, and consists almost exclusively of the small *Miconia robinsoniana* tree sheltering numerous ferns and mosses, particularly *Lycopodium;* and (7) the pampa zone, or grasslands, which covers the highest area of the island, where long periods of wind and fog prevent the growth of any of the native Galápagos trees, and which gives way to rolling expanses of bracken with occasional tree ferns of the genus *Cyathea.*

The Galápagos Biota

Mammals

The mammals are represented predominantly by marine forms, the most notable of which are the pinnipeds. The fur seal originated in sub-Antarctic regions, while the sea lion is a descendant of the California sea lion. Several species of whales and porpoises are also commonly seen among the islands. Of the terrestrial mammals two are bats; the remainder consists of six species of rice rats, though four of these have become extinct because of the introduction of black rats on the islands where they existed.

Land Birds

There are relatively few resident land birds in the islands and the majority are endemic. Among the birds are three predators (two owls and one hawk), and the notorious Darwin's finches, a group of thirteen closely related, innocuous little gray birds distributed throughout the entire archipelago, with as many as ten or eleven different species found together on some of the larger islands. Each species has evolved a beak of distinctive shape and size, permitting it to make use of a specific type of food, thus minimizing competition. Some marked extremes in the group are the insectivorous warbler finch, the seed-cracking large ground finch, the tool-using woodpecker finch, and the leaf-eating vegetarian finch. Another interesting land bird is the Galápagos rail, a secretive little bird that lives in the undergrowth and has almost completely lost its ability to fly.

Seabirds

Large numbers of seabirds can be seen in the Galápagos. Many of these are highly pelagic species that use the islands solely for the purpose of nesting. Nesting activities are visible at all times of year, but the birds can be grouped into three main categories according to their reproductive cycles. First are those species that nest at a fixed time each year, such as the great frigate and the waved albatross. These probably take advantage of some seasonal improvement in their food supply and may also make use of the concentrated timing to regroup from their scattered ocean wanderings. The second group comprises birds that nest at fixed intervals shorter than a year in length. This group is well-exhibited by the swallow-tailed gull and the Audubon shearwater in which individuals begin their cycle every nine or ten months. Since the entire population is not synchronized, nesting takes place all year round. The third type includes the birds that depend on fluctuating food resources and will nest whenever the conditions are good. The blue-footed booby is an excellent example of a species that will make haphazard attempts at breeding during any month, but will abandon an entire colony if the fish supply moves so far from the breeding grounds that adults cannot travel back and forth to feed their young.

Reptiles

In this isolated ecosystem, largely cut off from the major populations of land vertebrates on earth, reptiles have come to occupy a prominent position. The lava lizards are the top insectivores; the three nonpoisonous species of snakes represent one of only two types of second-level predators; the marine iguanas exploit an extreme, unprecedented niche; and the giant tortoises, like living fossils, maintain an archaic place as the only native grazers.

Terrestrial Invertebrates

The invertebrates of the Galápagos are generally not very obvious. As in other island situations, the insect life presents a fairly high proportion of flightlessness. Since there are few diurnal butterflies, the flowers of endemic plants are usually small and inconspicuous. The land snails, almost all of which belong to one genus, show a large number of species, with many different local variations, particularly on Santa Cruz Island. They are found on practically all islands and in every habitat.

Flora

The plant community of the Galápagos is regarded as highly disharmonic compared to the flora on the mainland of South America. This means that the composition of the vegetation does not show a normal proportion between the different types of plants. Ferns, composites, grasses, and sedges are dominant over the other forms, whereas tree-forming types are poorly represented. This situation is largely due to the fact that large trees tend to produce heavy seeds that are not suited for long-range dispersal. As a result several plants of typically shrubby or herbaceous tendencies have evolved into arboreal forms.

Marine Life

Because of the predominance of cold ocean currents flowing through the Galápagos Islands the marine life is not truly tropical. There are few coral formations and no warm-water coral reef communities. Instead rich growths of algae (seaweed) are common. The fish as well as the invertebrates represent a mixture of warm- and cold-water types, of which a high 20 to 25 percent are endemic.

Conservation in the Galápagos

Human Impact

Although the Galápagos remained untouched by man until fairly recently, the effects of his short presence in the islands have been disastrous upon their fragile ecosystem.

First the pirates of the seventeenth and eighteenth centuries, and then the whalers and sealers of the nineteenth, carried off hundreds of thousands of giant tortoises to store as a source of fresh meat aboard ship. At the same time they introduced various types of mammals that established themselves on a number of islands. Some, such as rats, disembarked involuntarily from the sailing ships, while others, like goats, were intentionally set free in order to provide these early sailors with meat.

In 1832 the islands were claimed by Ecuador, and with their annexation came the first permanent settlers. It was only natural that these colonists, as well as later settlers, would bring with them a thorough stock of domestic animals, as well as many other living organisms that they transported unknowingly. As a result, the majority of the islands today carry an assortment of these relics, including cattle, horses, donkeys, pigs, goats, dogs, cats, rats, mice, and many introduced insects and plants. In many places these have caused severe damage to the native flora and fauna. Most gravely affected by predation from pigs and dogs were the tortoises, land iguanas, and dark-rumped (or Hawaiian) petrels. Unable to resist pressure from the introduced black rats, four out of six species of endemic rice rats have become extinct. Also, on a number of islands goats and other herbivores have seriously altered the native vegetation. Among the major islands only Tower and Fernandina have completely escaped such introductions so far.

The Galápagos National Park

Recognizing the international importance of preserving the Galápagos archipelago in as natural a state as possible, the Ecuadorian government designated all uninhabited areas of the islands as its first national park in 1959. A few years later a fledgling park administration was set up. Today it comprises a staff of sixty conservation administrators and park wardens who carry out a number of programs involving tourist control, eradication of introduced species, captive breeding of the endangered species, and education of Galápagos inhabitants.

The Charles Darwin Research Station

Simultaneously with the creation of the Galápagos National Park the Charles Darwin Foundation for the Galápagos Islands was established with the support of UNESCO and various other international organizations. Its purpose was to focus attention on the plight of the Galápagos biota and to raise money internationally for its preservation. Under its direction the Charles Darwin Research Station was set up on Santa Cruz Island to carry out the following objectives: advise and guide the Galápagos National Park Administration during its formative years, prompt and support scientific investigation, help establish the conservation programs in collaboration with the national park administration, advise the national park administration on scientific matters, and appeal internationally for Galápagos conservation funds on a sustained basis. Over the years the station has gained worldwide recognition for its efforts.

Resident Galápagos Vertebrates

Appendix II

Mammals

Fur Seal *Arctocephalus australis galapagoensis*
Sea Lion *Zalophus californianus wollebaeki*
Bat *Lasiurus brachyotis*
Bat *Lasiurus cinereus*
Fernandina Rice Rat *Nesoryzomis narboroughi*
Barringon Rice Rat *Oryzomis bauri*

Seabirds

Galápagos Penguin *Spheniscus mendiculus*
Waved Albatross *Diomedea irrorata*
Hawaiian (Dark-rumped) Petrel *Pterodroma phaeopygia*
Audubon's Shearwater *Puffinus lherminieri*
White-vented (Elliot's) Petrel *Oceanites gracilis*
Wedge-rumped (Galápagos) Storm Petrel *Oceanodroma tethys*
Band-rumped (Madeiran) Petrel *Oceanodroma castro*
Red-billed Tropic Bird *Phaethon aetherous*
Brown Pelican *Pelecanus occidentalis*
Blue-footed Booby *Sula nebouxii*
Masked (White) Booby *Sula dactylatra*
Red-footed Booby *Sula sula*
Flightless Cormorant *Nannopterum harrisi*
Magnificent Frigate Bird *Fregata magnificens*
Great Frigate Bird *Fregata minor*
Great Blue Heron *Ardea herodias*
Common Egret *Casmerodius albus*
Yellow-crowned Night Heron *Nyctanassa violacea*
Lava (Galápagos Green) Heron *Butorides sundevalli*
Flamingo *Phoenicopterurs ruber*
White-cheeked (Bahama) Pintail *Anas bahamensis*
Oystercatcher *Haematopus ostralegus*
Common Stilt *Himantopus himantopus*
Lava (Dusky) Gull *Larus fuliginosus*
Swallow-tailed Gull *Creagrus furcatus*
Sooty Tern *Sterna fuscata*
Brown Noddy *Anous stolidus*

Land Birds

Galápagos Hawk *Buteo galapagoensis*
Galápagos Rail, or Crake *Laterullus spilonotus*
Paint-billed Crake *Neocrex erythrops*
Galápagos Dove *Zenaida galapagoensis*
Dark-billed Cuckoo *Coccyzus melanocoryphus*
Barn Owl *Tyto alba*
Short-eared Owl *Asio flammeus*
Vermilion Flycatcher *Pyrocephalus rubinus*
Large-billed Flycatcher *Myiarchus magnirostris*
Galápagos Martin *Progne modesta*
Galápagos Mockingbird *Nesomimus parvulus*
San Cristóbal Mockingbird *Nesomimus melanotis*
Hood Mockingbird *Nesomimus macdonaldi*
Floreana Mockingbird *Nesomimus trifasciatus*
Yellow Warbler *Dendroica petechia*
Small Ground Finch *Geospiza fuliginosa*
Medium Ground Finch *Geospiza fortis*
Sharp-beaked Ground Finch *Geospiza difficilis*
Cactus Finch *Geospiza scandens*
Large Cactus Finch *Geospiza conirostris*
Vegetarian Finch *Platyspiza crassirostris*
Small Tree Finch *Camarhynchus parvulus*
Medium Tree Finch *Camarhynchus pauper*
Large Tree Finch *Camarhynchus psittacula*
Woodpecker Finch *Camarhynchus pallidus*
Mangrove Finch *Camarhynchus heliobates*
Warbler Finch *Certhidea olivacea*

Reptiles

Galápagos Tortoise *Geochelone elephantopus*
Marine Iguana *Amblyrhnynchus cristatus*
Galápagos Land Iguana *Conolophus subcristatus*
Barrington Land Iguana *Conolophus pallidus*
Lava Lizards *Tropidurus* spp.
Snakes *Dromicus* spp.
Geckos *Phyllodactylus* spp.

Photographic Notes

Appendix III

It is probably not surprising that someone who grew up in the Galápagos Islands took to nature photography. As a child I became gradually aware of the wonders that surrounded me. I was intimately familiar with the lives of many plants and animals, but not until the age of ten or so did I begin to feel their deep significance. I went from taking everything around me for granted to rediscovering an astonishing world.

When I was twelve I spent long hours in the midst of a courting colony of blue-footed boobies, and at one point I suddenly made a decision: I would make a complete collection of photographs of the life cycle of each of the seabirds in the Galápagos. Little did I realize that fourteen years and twelve thousand transparencies later this project would still be incomplete.

I had already experimented from time to time with my father's small Kodak camera and black-and-white film and had acquired a great interest for what could be done with this. But I found out that in order to achieve my goal I would need a single-lens reflex camera, and thus I began selling goat skins and other mementos to the few tourists who visited the islands at that time. However, I did not consciously intend to become a photographer; I was simply fascinated by all free-living things, and taking pictures was to me the only sure way of bringing a small part of nature home with me.

When later I began taking my first "real" photographs I realized at once that this was not just a casual hobby for me. Photography quickly became my way of life, the dominant purpose of all my trips. I learned slowly, by trial and error, many technical details, such as that the quality of sunlight is softer early and late in the day, or that on cloudy days I should avoid including sea or sky in my shots, for these would inevitably look bleached out. My learning was often slowed tremendously by the long delays in getting my color film processed in the United States; sometimes it would be six months or more before a roll was returned. But eventually I gained a feeling for my subjects because I knew them so well, and I was often able to sense intuitively when a shot would be outstanding.

Still, I considered my photography a personal affair, and it was most reluctantly, at the age of seventeen, that I agreed to write my first article on the giant tortoises of Alcedo Crater. Only with the writing of this book did it dawn on me that nature photography and writing would be my career.

When I was trying to decide which camera to acquire, most people advised me to get a Nikon, which was reputed to be by far the most reliable professional brand. Then a very kind man making a film in the islands generously gave me an excellent camera made by Pentax that he had been using for years. It was an old model, but gave superb results. Now, after three other Pentax cameras have served me faithfully through rain, salt spray, sand, a few falls, and every other kind of hardship, I would not give up their light weight, maneuverability, and ruggedness for anything.

On almost all my trips by boat or in the back country I carry an assortment of five lenses: 24 mm, 35 mm, 50 mm macro, 135 mm, and 300 mm. These are all easy to hand-hold and provide the full range necessary to capture virtually every aspect of the Galápagos. They have slow f stops, f/3.5 or even f/5.6, because I have found that shots taken at a wider aperture do not offer the depth of field I desire, and since fast lenses are heavier, this would be a drawback rather than an advantage on many backpacking trips. For the same reason I do not use a tripod, preferring the versatility and quickness of action made possible by a hand-held camera.

My entire outfit, plus a half dozen rolls of film, polarizing filters, extension tubes (and matches, pen and paper, needles and fish hooks), fits into a case 30 by 22 by 12 centimeters that my father designed for me. It is made of thin plywood with a neoprene rubber gasket, which means it is fully waterproof. Every lens fits into a small compartment cushioned with foam rubber. The shoulder strap is fastened in the middle of the sides of the box instead of at the corners, which allows it to swivel into an upright position when opened without my having to unload it. This lets me change film or lenses in virtually any situation—hiking (I can keep on walking provided there are not too many rocks in the path!), standing at the railing of a boat in rough seas, or even perched in a tree. Because the wood is insulated and painted white on the outside, the box can sit in the sun for hours without the contents becoming dangerously heated (as a side benefit, the box can be used to reflect light when a shaded subject needs subtle illumination). I have used it in rain, disembarked with it through heavy surf, and even swam across the mile-long caldera lake of Fernandina Island with it in tow. All in all, it is virtually shockproof, heatproof, and waterproof. Many times I would have either lost or damaged my equipment—or been forced not to risk using it—had it not been for this handy gadget. Complete, it weighs ten pounds and fits in front of me so that I do not have to add to the weight and bulk of my backpack, which in these waterless islands is heavy and bulky enough.

My favorite film is Kodachrome 64 for its faithful color reproduction and sharp definition. I do not like artificial lighting and always try to exploit natural light to a maximum degree. As these plates may testify, I try to use the light of day to add a special mood to the scene, beyond the simple documentation of the subject. This of course requires timing and luck. I do not consider photography strenuous work but rather a matter of being on the spot at the right moment. Perhaps most important is the ability to sense when this right moment has come.

I have never been interested in the mechanics of photography, and feel that to be a successful photographer one does not need to study the technicalities of film and shutter speed (these details come soon enough with practice) but rather to be in touch with one's surroundings, to be sensitive to the quality of the light, the level of the clouds, the wind on the water, the shadows of the trees—in other words, the small, often unnoticed characteristics that enrich the scene.

In ten years nature photography has become my vehicle for communicating my views to other people. I hope to use it to contribute to the awareness that nature should be respected and valued at all levels for what it is in itself, not just for what use may be made of it by man.

The following notes are expanded versions of the captions to the color plates in this book.

Front-matter plates:

I. With a rainstorm in the distance and bright sunlight in the foreground, the contrast of colors along the Bartolomé beach was enhanced by using a polarizing filter to cut down on some of the reflection on the water. *Takumar 24 mm.*

II. In the heart of the rainy season the afternoon sun shines softly on the tender grass cropped close to the ground by the grazing tortoises. Fumaroles are steaming in the distance. *Takumar 24 mm.*

III. While shredded clouds blow over the caldera of Alcedo in the rainy season, an intrigued hawk alights near steaming fumaroles for a better look at the photographer. *Takumar 24 mm.*

IV. As the incoming tide and heavy surf pound the lava shoreline, a marine iguana returns from a feeding foray. *Takumar 24 mm.*

V. On the rim of Fernandina a male land iguana pauses near the edge of a caldera one thousand meters deep. *Takumar 24 mm.*

Plates beginning on page 57:

1. Fumarole steam and morning clouds mix to fill the caldera of Alcedo with mist while the opposite rim remains clear. The entire scene is bathed in the golden tone of sunrise. *Takumar 24 mm. Photo by Gil De Roy.*
2. In 1978, as soon as it had news of an eruption inside the caldera of Fernandina, the Charles Darwin Research Station sent a party to investigate. When we arrived at the caldera lake a week later, the activity had died, but fresh lava that had entered the lake was still steaming profusely. *Takumar 135 mm.*
3. On its twelfth day of life the 1979 volcanic eruption at the base of Cerro Azul belches gasses and lava in great fountains and a ribbon of cooling lava flows downslope. The last light of dusk illuminates the surrounding landscape in this scene taken from an extinct cone eight hundred meters away. *Macro-Takumar 50 mm.*
4. Against the red glow of the atmosphere and the roar of escaping gasses, a time exposure of several minutes reveals the path of lava bombs as graceful arcs of light. *Takumar 135 mm.*
5. At dusk the glow of the eruption is reflected in the heat cloud forming above the vents. *Takumar 35 mm.*

6. After several days of rain and miserable weather, one clear morning finally reveals the caldera of Cerro Azul in all its splendor. *Takumar 24 mm.*

7, 8. Lava flows and cinder formations attest to Cerro Azul's ongoing activity. *Takumar 135 mm.*

9. In 1978 a new eruption again poured lava into the Fernandina lake. When we arrived at the rim two days later, the entire surface of the lake was still steaming from the heat. *Takumar 35 mm.*

10. As the morning sun slowly penetrates the caldera, stillness prevails on the shaded lake, as if a piece of night's calm were trapped inside the huge pit. *Takumar 24 mm.*

11. Surrounded by high walls, the caldera lake of Fernandina shimmers in the bluish morning light. *Takumar 135 mm.*

12. Seen from the rim of Volcan Alcedo, the rounded volcano of Fernandina rises into dark rain-seasoned clouds. *Takumar 83 mm.*

13. The golden light of sunrise filters through the morning haze to highlight a collection of sea lions, marine iguanas, flightless cormorant, and pelican at the base of the towering volcano of Fernandina. *Takumar 135 mm.*

14. This direct view into the steaming vent of an active fumarole reveals fragile sulfur crystals formed by precipitating hot gases. To obtain this shot I had to focus and snap the picture before steam fogged the lens. *Macro-Takumar 50 mm.*

15. Highlighted by the brilliant morning sunlight, sulfur crystals build delicate formations that slowly accumulate and crumble in constant succession around fumarole vents.

16. Having just risen over the rim of Alcedo, the sun shines fleetingly through a dense, contorting jet of fumarole steam. *Takumar 24 mm.*

17. Since water is scarce on the sunny rim of Fernandina during the cool season, doves seek out droplets of steam that precipitate on ferns and sedges growing around fumarole vents. *Takumar 135 mm.*

18. As I was recording this sunset view of Fernandina from a traveling boat, a diving blue-footed booby appeared just in time for a silhouette. *Takumar 135 mm.*

19, 23, 26, 27, 28. With late afternoon sunlight enhancing its metallic sheen, the Sullivan Bay lava flow comes to life in every detail of its formation.

20. Overcast skies give a bluish tinge to the dark lava flows streaking the flank of Volcan Wolf. It takes ten hours of hiking over jagged lava to reach the highest point in the Galápagos—seventeen hundred meters.

21. While the sulfur fumaroles of Volcan de Azufre inside the volcano of Sierra Negra disgorge steam in great billows, dew drops hang suspended in spider webs on the caldera floor. *Takumar 24 mm.*

22. The grazing light of sunrise accentuates the relief formed by recent lava flows cascading along the steep walls of the caldera of Cerro Azul. *Vivitar 300 mm.*

24. Touched only by sparse vegetation, the two tuff cones of James Bay retain their symmetrical shapes. This bright morning is typical of the warm season. *Takumar 24 mm.*

25. Some fingerlike protrusions of the ropy pahoehoe lava are called lava toes. *Macro-Takumar 50 mm.*

29. Seen from the steep eastern slope of Volcan Wolf, many recent lava flows create overlapping patterns extending toward the shoreline. *Macro-Takumar 50 mm.*

30. Even during the dry season the tiny *Mollugo* manages to bloom on the nearly sterile lava.

31. As far as the eye can see there is no trace of life—only heaped lava and scoria cones. The shadows of passing clouds add perspective to the mineral landscape. *Takumar 135 mm.*

32. As though it were still in motion, the glazed, bluish lava of the last century dribbles over an older, eroded terrain. *Takumar 50 mm.*

33. Though I have walked over the Sullivan Bay pahoehoe dozens of times, on each visit I discover new details, such as this pioneering *Brachycereus* cactus. *Takumar 135 mm.*

34. An untold number of centuries ago *Brachycereus* cacti grew in this spot, as is recorded in this lava mold in a place washed by the sea in Darwin Bay. *Macro-Takumar 50 mm.*

35. *Brachycereus* cacti find their ideal habitat in the lava wastelands. With the degradation of the terrain, other plants will take root and this species will inevitably disappear. *Takumar 24 mm.*

36. Growing on bare lava, the *Brachycereus* rarely blooms, and then only at night. This flower taken at dawn is already partially closed. *Takumar 135 mm. with extension tube.*

37. Seashells and sea urchins, barnacles and huge coral heads, attest to the cataclysmic events that occurred when the entire bay of Urvina rose out of the sea through geologic force. Twenty-five years later some vegetation has taken root among the sun-bleached remains of these marine organisms. *Takumar 24 mm.*

38. Many of the arid-zone plants lose their leaves during the dry season, but the *Erythrina* tree is decked in bright red flowers. *Takumar 24 mm.*
39. A spot of sun highlights a clump of *Opuntia* cacti inside the arid crater of Pinzon Island; hanging pads of the cacti are frayed by the high-reaching saddleback tortoises. *Takumar 35 mm.*
40. The cactus flowers on Champion Island are yellow when freshly open, then turn red with age. *Takumar 24 mm.*
41. Just before the onset of the rainy season the cacti burst into bloom; here the *Opuntia* flowers. *Takumar 135 mm.*
42. The early-morning blossoms of the *Jasminocereus* cactus. *Takumar 135 mm.*
43. Whereas many *Opuntia* cactus blossoms are damaged and torn by the feeding habits of Darwin's cactus finches, these flowers are still intact. *Takumar 83 mm.*
44. Using a wide-angle lens and underexposing by several stops, I obtained this shot of cactus silhouetted against the afternoon sky. *Takumar 24 mm.*
45. The *Scalesia* shrubs on Pinzon remain green even during the dry season. *Takumar 135 mm.*
46. Having shed their seeds, the dry flowers of *Scalesia villosa* remain perfect. *Takumar 83 mm. with extension tube.*
47. On the slope of an old tuff cone *Bursera* ("palo santo") trees stand leafless during the cool dry season. *Takumar 135 mm.*
48. Well into the dry season the *Sesuvium* plants of the Plazas have turned a deep red from lack of water. Clouds that produce only occasional drizzle hang low over the ocean. *Macro-Takumar 50.*
49. From the glittering sand dunes of Bartolomé grow the drought-loving *Tiquilia* (*Coldenia*). *Takumar 135 mm.*
50. Barely affected by drought, this euphorb blooms on sandy beaches or dusty slopes. *Takumar 135 mm. with extension tube.*
51. Not a winter scene but salt deposits in an old crater at James Bay with *Bursera* and *Erythrina* during the dry season. *Takumar 135 mm.*
52. Close-up of the tiny *Cordia leucophlyctis* flower. *Macro-Takumar 50 mm. with extension tube.*
53, 58. Spurred by the first heavy rains, the gray *Portulaca* that blanket Plazas suddenly cover themselves with delicate flowers every afternoon before sunset. *Takumar 24 mm. and Macro-Takumar 50 mm.*
54. Endemic tomatoes bloom in many of the driest regions of the islands. *Takumar 135 mm. with extension tube.*
55. Though it is leafless in the middle of the dry season, the *Erythrina* produces brilliant flowers. *Takumar 135 mm.*
56. As a protection against desiccation, the coastal *Scalesia* of Floreana is covered with fine hair. *Takumar 135 mm.*
57. Long after most other annual plants have died following the rainy season, this morning glory still unfolds its delicate flowers over the parched lava. *Macro-Takumar 50 mm.*
59. Brilliant morning sun highlights ferns and mosses on the rim of Alcedo. *Takumar 135 mm.*
60. In the damp shade of the *Scalesia* forest a small vine reaches up a mossy trunk. *Takumar 135 mm.*
61. In one of the highest vegetation zones on Santa Cruz a rich variety of epiphytic ferns and mosses is sustained by the cloud forest atmosphere. *Takumar 50 mm.*
62. The typical misty weather in the highlands of Santa Cruz enhances the colors of the ferns and mosses. *Macro-Takumar 50 mm.*
63. In temporary ponds where tortoises come to wallow, the delicate *Ludwigia* blossoms. *Takumar 135 mm.*
64. An epiphytic bromeliad collects water and nutrients in its core rather than by its roots. *Takumar 135 mm.*
65. Cloudy weather gives the *Tournefortia* leaves a waxy look. *Takumar 135 mm.*
66. In the warm rainy season sun and clouds play games over the highlands of Santa Cruz. The *Scalesia* forest creeps up the northern slopes of the hills, where it is sheltered from the wind. *Takumar 50 mm.*
67. In the moist grasslands of Santa Cruz Island tree ferns overlook the *Scalesia* forest and, in the distance, the arid coastline. *Macro-Takumar 50 mm.*
68. As the first sun rays pierce the clouds, this dawn-blooming morning glory begins to wilt. *Takumar 135 mm.*
69. Rainwater ponds in the high grasslands are frequently covered with floating *Azolla* ferns that turn bright red where they are fully exposed to the light. *Macro-Takumar 50 mm.*
70. The island's wettest area, the miconia zone on Santa Cruz may receive more than two meters of rain and fog drip in a year. *Macro-Takumar 135 mm.*
71, 80. In the highland forest of Santa Cruz a male vermilion flycatcher pauses briefly to in-

spect the low foliage for insects. *Takumar 135 mm.*

72. While hiking along the rim of Alcedo I spotted this hidden moth on a foggy day. *Takumar 83 mm.*
73. A large spider devours a cockroach it has caught. Taken with a strobe on the lava-rock wall of our kitchen. *Macro-Takumar 50 mm.*
74. Surrounded by shimmering raindrops, a spider has just finished spinning its web among the golden spines of a cactus. *Takumar 83 mm with extension tube.*
75. Having burned away the morning fog, the sun glitters in the suspended dew drops in this spider web. *Takumar 83 mm.*
76. A ray of afternoon sun illuminates the underside of a fern where these endemic land snails wander. *Macro-Takumar 50 mm.*
77. Silhouetted against the noonday filtered sun, a grasshopper gnaws on a *Scalesia* flower. *Takumar 135 mm.*
78. The sun filters through the mangrove foliage onto a pair of yellow warblers tending their nest. Chicken feathers and cotton threads show that this nest was built near human habitations. *Takumar 135 mm. with extension tube.*
79. The endemic large-billed flycatcher is very curious about people and therefore easy to photograph. *Takumar 135 mm.*
81. The texture and color of a female vermilion flycatcher perched in low shrubs nearly match those of the damp mosses. *Takumar 135 mm. with extension tube.*
82. During the rainy season on Volcan Alcedo a freshly hatched moth dries its wings in the morning warmth. *Macro-Takumar 50 mm.*
83. On islands where there are no hawks to compete for food, short-eared owls are diurnal as well as nocturnal. This owl caught an introduced mouse late in the afternoon in the *Scalesia* forest and brought it to its mate at a prospective nest site underneath a low bush. *Takumar 135 mm.*
84. A rare find: hidden in a dense clump of grass a pair of Galápagos rails sit together briefly on the nest during an incubation changeover. A morning of patient sitting accustomed these shy birds to my presence. *Takumar 135 mm. with extension tube and strobe.*
85. Secretive and almost flightless, a Galápagos rail and its young huddle among tall *Lycopodium* mosses in the humid miconia zone of Santa Cruz. *Takumar 135 mm.*
86. I took this shot from a small skiff while rowing into a mangrove inlet where rays and turtles glide in the calm water. *Macro-Takumar 50 mm.*
87. Photographed with a polarizing filter to diminish the reflections on the water, a school of rays becomes visible as it glides through a quiet mangrove lagoon.
88. As the intrigued turtle slowly circled the small skiff, I got this picture without having to use a polarizing filter, which would have cut out the blurred reflection of the mangrove foliage. *Takumar 83 mm.*
89. Trying to catch a breaking wave coincidentally with the passing of a blue-footed booby was a patience-straining experience. *Vivitar 300 mm.*
90. With each new wave roaring into a sea cave, then shooting upward through a crevice in the ceiling, the Hood Island blow hole resembles a geyser. I took many shots of the sun through the jet of water and each one came out differently. *Takumar 24 mm.*
91. The sight of porpoises cavorting around the bow of a traveling boat is an endless source of fascination for tourists as well as for people like myself who have watched them hundreds of times. On a flat, calm, warm-season day a bottle-nosed dolphin barely produces a ripple as he breaks the mirror surface of the sea. *Takumar 135 mm.*

92, 98. Filtered sunlight gives a velvety look to both landscape and sea.

93. With Fernandina's great active volcano looming in the background, penguins, marine iguanas, and sea lions coexist peacefully on the rugged lava shores. *Takumar 24 mm.*
94. I was trying to capture the crystal clarity of the water with a polarizing filter when this group of young sea lions glided by. *Takumar 24 mm.*
95. A sea lion hauls up on the beach of Punta Espinosa during the brief appearance of the sun on a cloudy afternoon. *Macro-Takumar 50 mm.*
96. Unusually clear water reveals the rocky bottom in front of a high cliff on Bainbridge Island. *Macro-Takumar 50 mm.*
97. On a typical morning during the cool season low shredded clouds hang over the sea around Devil's Crown near Floreana Island. *Takumar 135 mm.*
99. Shortly before the appearance of the sun the dawn light faintly reveals fresh tracks of a sea turtle that came up onto the beach to nest at night. *Takumar 35 mm.*
100. The sea appears silver as the sun sinks beyond the pinnacle of Bartolomé, seen from

the summit of the small island. *Takumar 135 mm.*

101. My impulsive decision to hike over a shoreline tuff cone rather than around it was rewarded with this view of eddies in the ocean currents shimmering under the sun. *Takumar 24 mm.*
102. The orange light of sunset gives relief to every detail of the pinnacle of Bartolomé. *Macro-Takumar 50 mm.*
103. The first rays of sunrise flood the landscape with golden tones, as seen from the summit of Bartolomé. *Takumar 24 mm.*
104. Cold ocean upwellings produce a calm blanket of fog on the shores of Fernandina at sunrise. Dozens of marine iguanas, as well as a lava heron, await the warmth of the sun. *Takumar 24 mm.*
105. From a high cliff sea lion tracks are visible on this small beach. The white sand is made mostly of corals and seashells. *Takumar 135 mm.*
106. A lava beach is as black as the lava from which it was formed. *Takumar 24 mm.*
107. Some spatter and volcanic scoria cones are bright red instead of black and, when eroded, produce beaches of that color.
108. A beach made from eroded tuff is orange in color and glitters with minute crystals when seen up close.
109. Like a ribbon emerging from the sea, marine iguanas slowly make their way up a lava-sand beach to their sleeping spot above the high-tide limit. *Takumar 24 mm.*
110. An iguana returning from a feeding trip emerges from the water to blend perfectly with its surroundings. *Takumar 135 mm.*
111. Feeding marine iguanas cling to the rocks as the rising tide washes over them. *Takumar 135 mm.*
112. Marine iguanas congregate in fantastic densities to bask in their favorite sunning spots. On this most-photographed rock at Punta Espinosa the morning sun glitters on their spiny crests. *Takumar 135 mm.*
113. Morning sunlight outlines the crest of a basking marine iguana among dozens of its kind. *Takumar 135 mm.*
114. A marine iguana on his way to feed swims through the clear water of a grotto at James Bay. *Takumar 135 mm.*
115. At the instant I snapped this iguana's picture he licked the rock briefly in an apparently territorial display. *Takumar 135 mm.*
116. Only once have I witnessed the peak of the marine iguanas' nesting season, which lasted less than a week. Dozens of females milled about on the sand above the high-tide limit, fighting over nesting spots or partially dug burrows. *Takumar 135 mm.*
117. A Hood Island iguana crops off the short covering of algae in a tide pool. *Takumar 135 mm.*
118. The breeding colors of the male Hood Island iguana are acquired shortly before the beginning of the warm season and fade back to duller tones after mating. *Takumar 135 mm.*
119. A colorful Hood Island iguana is oblivious of the sally light-foot crabs clambering over him, perhaps pulling off an occasional tick. *Takumar 135 mm.*
120. A brightly colored marine iguana male on Hood Island bobs his head in aggression among the darker females. *Takumar 135 mm.*
121. A convenient lookout for flies: a male lava lizard perches on the head of basking marine iguanas. *Takumar 135 mm.*
122. Dwarfed by the strong claws of a marine iguana, a young lava lizard remains alert to the movement of a fly. *Takumar 135 mm. with extension tube.*
123. The marine iguanas on Isabela Island are the largest of the race, the males weighing well over fifteen pounds. *Takumar 135 mm.*
124. While feeding on the short green algae covering the rocks, marine iguanas hang tight as showers of spray from the Hood Island blow hole envelop them. *Takumar 135 mm.*
125. Occasionally, lizards are seen catching and devouring young of their own species. This cannibalism may help to control the population density, which is so heavy that every available space in an adequate terrain is always occupied. *Takumar 135 mm.*
126. A female lizard endemic to Hood Island is larger than the lizards on the other islands and has more red on her head and chest. *Takumar 135 mm. with extension tube.*
127. A predator that sometimes turns prey, the lava lizard makes a quick job of dismantling a large grasshopper. *Takumar 135 mm.*
128. A male lava lizard surveys his territory from atop a prominent rock. *Takumar 135 mm.*
129. A marine iguana basks in the sun while a lava lizard looks out for flies and a small Darwin's finch inspects it for blood-filled ticks. *Takumar 135 mm.*
130. A female lava lizard in her brightest coloration during the rainy season stares into the lens of the camera. *Macro-Takumar 50 mm.*
131. Two male lava lizards engage in a serious territorial fight atop the plastic shutter of our window. *Takumar 135 mm.*
132. After a rainy night a lava lizard has just

emerged to bask in the sun. The special light effect was obtained by photographing the lizard through a bush laden with drops of water. *Takumar 135 mm.*

133. Only on rare occasions have I left my camera on board the boat while guiding a group of tourists on the islands. When on one such day this snake proceeded to catch and eat a lizard before our eyes, a very kind lady came to my rescue by lending me her camera.
134. Three species of endemic snakes, with many island subspecies, inhabit Galápagos; none is poisonous and all kill their prey by coiling around it. *Takumar 135 mm.*
135. Moments after catching a male lava lizard, a Galápagos snake begins swallowing it head first while still coiled around its body.
136. In an area where people are rarely seen, this male land iguana was inflating his throat threateningly and getting ready to flee into the underbrush when this picture was taken. *Takumar 135 mm.*
137. During the month of October, with cool sunny weather prevailing inside the caldera of Fernandina, iguana hatchlings in camouflage coloration elude Galápagos hawks on their way to vegetated zones. *Takumar 135 mm.*
138. This picture was taken shortly before packs of feral dogs eliminated all the wild populations of land iguanas on Santa Cruz Island in 1975. *Takumar 135 mm.*
139. From the rim of Fernandina it is a one-thousand-meter plunge to the mineral lake rippled by the morning breeze. Prevailing winds from the southeast drive shredded clouds over the rim of the caldera, while the remainder of the summit is almost always sunny. *Takumar 24 mm.*
140. Seen through a clump of grass, a male land iguana wanders like some prehistoric reptile on his morning foraging trip. *Photo by Jacqueline De Roy.*
141. A very unusual sight: a congenial group of land iguanas on the rim of Fernandina, consisting of several females and at least one male. Normally, their aggressive nature prevents such close associations. *Takumar 135 mm.*
142. When the *Portulaca* blooms in the late afternoon during the brief rainy season, land iguanas wander from plant to plant to pluck the sweet yellow flowers. *Takumar 135 mm.*
143. Fighting males approach each other in a three-quarter frontal position, bobbing their heads threateningly and lunging for each other's necks again and again. *Takumar 135 mm.*
144. Extending their legs stiffly to allow better access, land iguanas permit finches and mockingbirds to clean them of blood-filled ticks. Here a mockingbird holds a piece of shredded skin instead. *Photo by Andre De Roy. Takumar 135 mm.*
145. After roughly scratching off the spines, an iguana on the rim of Fernandina bites into a juicy fallen cactus pad that provides him with necessary moisture. *Takumar 135 mm.*
146. With the shady blue interior of the caldera as a backdrop, a land iguana makes an appearance over the rim of the Fernandina volcano. *Takumar 135 mm.*
147. It required a fair amount of crawling beneath a thorn bush to photograph this land iguana heading for its hiding place. *Takumar 135 mm.*
148. Enveloped in fumarole steam, tortoises wander from their nighttime pool on the rim of Alcedo Volcano on their morning foraging trip. Patience and luck enabled me to snap this picture during one brief instant when the wind cleared the steam around the walking tortoise. *Takumar 24 mm.*
149. A giant tortoise stands rigidly in an outstretched position to allow a small Darwin's finch to rid it of ticks. *Takumar 135 mm.*
150. As a light breeze under the sun's first rays stirs clouds and steam within the caldera of Alcedo, a hawk uses an immobile tortoise for a perch.
151. Walking in a thick, muddy wallow, a tortoise casts both a shadow and a reflection.
152. After days of rain and cloudy weather inside the Alcedo caldera, the sun broke through and bathed the scene with golden rays one late afternoon. *Takumar 24 mm.*
153. A consummate grazer, an Alcedo tortoise crops weeds and grass close to the ground. *Vivitar 300 mm.*
154. Crouched under a dense bush, I managed to keep my camera dry long enough to catch a few shots of a sudden torrential downpour during the warm season on Alcedo volcano. *Takumar 135 mm.*
155. The seasonal rains have ceased and the temporary ponds on Alcedo are shrinking. For a week I camped with my family in this spot and watched every afternoon as the giant tortoises converged from the surrounding grazing meadows to drink and settle to sleep in the warm, muddy wallows. *Takumar 24 mm.*
156. In an area devoid of plants because of fumarole activity, tortoises go through a ritualized threat display in a wallow. *Takumar 135 mm.*

157. I found this tortoise skeleton in an open pumice plain, far from its normal range around the vegetated summit of the volcano. It probably died from overheating. *Takumar 135 mm.*
158. The morning sun burns away the fog over a rain pond near the Alcedo steam vent.
159. As a rainbow announces the onset of the warm rainy season, tortoises everywhere in the caldera of Alcedo are busy mating. *Takumar 135 mm.*
160. Quite by chance I came upon these hatchling tortoises escaping from their nest on the caldera floor of Alcedo volcano in the heart of the dry season. *Takumar 135 mm.*
161. Under a blanket of fog that often fills the Alcedo caldera in the rainy season, tortoises mate in a field of pumice. *Takumar 135 mm.*
162. This sedentary old male tortoise lives alone inside the parched crater of Pinzon (Duncan) Island. He threatens people in the same manner he uses to threaten other tortoises: he raises his head and opens his sharp jaws. *Takumar 35 mm.*
163. In an open-air pen at the Charles Darwin Research Station on Santa Cruz Island, the last survivor of the Pinta Island tortoises awaits the meager chance that a mate might be discovered on his home island, where introduced goats and human plunderers appear to have brought his race to extinction. *Takumar 135 mm.*
164. Held captive in open-air pens on Santa Cruz Island, the last three Hood tortoise males are bred with the remaining eleven females in order to restock their home island. *Takumar 135 mm.*
165. Gulping great juicy chunks, a Pinzon tortoise devours a fallen cactus pad, often its only source of water during the dry months. *Takumar 135 mm.*
166, 167. Since saddleback tortoises are shyer and quicker than the domed types, it took patient stalking to catch one of these browsing individuals unaware. *Takumar 135 mm.*
168. On the rim of Volcan Alcedo a small ground finch ruffles his feathers on a damp morning. *Takumar 135 mm.*
169. All of Darwin's finches build dome-shaped nests, the ground finches mostly in cacti, the others sometimes in trees and shrubs. *Takumar 135 mm.*
170. When the *Erythrina* comes into bloom in October or November, several species of Darwin's finches take advantage of the flowers for food. Adult breeding birds of all species have a shiny black beak, nonbreeders show an orange or amber color, and young birds such as this one have a pale-yellow lower mandible. *Takumar 135 mm.*
171. The agile tree finch has access to food sources other finches are unable to reach. *Takumar 135 mm.*
172. The large ground finch (male) specializes in cracking very hard seeds that are unusable by the others. *Takumar 135 mm. with extension tube.*
173. The small ground finch (an immature male with almost-black plumage) typically feeds on small sedge and grass seeds. All ground finches (genus *Geospiza*) are mottled gray in females and young, black in adult males. *Takumar 135 mm. with extension tube.*
174. The sharp-beaked ground finch (male) has a more restricted range and feeds on small seeds, flowers, and insects. *Takumar 135 mm.*
175. With its long pointed beak the cactus finch prods deep into the *Opuntia* blossoms and also punctures the fruit for seeds. This pair shows well the color difference between male and female. *Takumar 135 mm.*
176. The large cactus finch (male) is restricted to the northern and southern islands, where the regular cactus finch does not exist. It may be a somewhat less specialized relict species that has been largely displaced by the more successful type. *Takumar 135 mm. with extension tube.*
177. The vegetarian finch is the largest and eats flowers, fruits, many leaves, and even lichens. *Takumar 135 mm.*
178. The small tree finch feeds on a variety of small insects, tiny flowers, buds, and fruits, and generally cleans up what the other finches overlook. Tree finches are black in color, with only the males of some species having black on the head or forward part of the body. *Takumar 135 mm.*
179. The large tree finch is found only in the high, humid parts of the islands, where it feeds on large sedentary insects and fruits. The medium tree finch is restricted to Floreana Island, where I have never seen or photographed it. *Takumar 135 mm.*
180. The woodpecker finch is perhaps the most remarkable, having adapted to feed much like a true woodpecker by hammering at dead branches to extract boring insects, and even using a cactus spine or twig as a tool in place of the woodpecker's extremely long, probing tongue. *Takumar 135 mm.*
181. The mangrove finch feeds similarly to the woodpecker finch, but its range is limited to the vast mangrove thickets along the western

shore of Isabela Island and on Fernandina Island. *Takumar 135 mm.*

182. The medium ground finch (female) eats a fair variety of medium-sized seeds, often found on the ground. *Takumar 135 mm.*
183. The warbler finch is another extreme that looks, behaves, and sings like a real warbler and feeds on small insects. *Takumar 135 mm.*
184. The mockingbird endemic to Floreana Island has become extinct on the main island, probably due to feral house cats taking advantage of the bird's ground-foraging habits, but survives on the small satellite islands around Floreana, such as Champion Island. *Takumar 135 mm.*
185. The Hood Island mockingbird, with a longer beak and larger feet than the others, is restricted to that island. *Takumar 135 mm.*
186. When I found this dove nesting inside an abandoned iguana burrow too dark to photograph, I used the white underside of my wooden camera box as a reflector. *Takumar 135 mm.*
187. The Galápagos mockingbird, here eating an endemic tomato on the rim of Fernandina, is found on all of the central and northern islands. *Takumar 135 mm.*
188. Concealed except for their eye-rings and feet, doves spend most of their time on the ground. *Takumar 135 mm.*
189. Many remnants of prehistoric as well as historic volcanic activity shape the caldera of Fernandina. *Macro-Takumar 50 mm.*

190–192. On a damp gray morning inside the caldera of Alcedo an immature Galápagos hawk arranges his feathers with great care. While waiting for the warmth of the sun to produce updrafts, sometimes three or four dozen hawks would sit around our camp, attracted by the unusual sight. *Takumar 135 mm.*

193. A hawk's nest on a lava outcropping increases in size each year as a new layer of branches is added by the birds. *Takumar 135 mm.*
194. Intrigued by the unusual presence of humans, an immature hawk comes down to perch close above my head. *Takumar 135 mm.*
195. As the morning sun penetrates into the caldera of Fernandina, a hawk takes advantage of the thermal updrafts along the steep wall. *Vivitar 300 mm.*
196. When the marine iguanas become sluggish from the drop in temperature with the coming of night, a hawk makes an easy kill. *Takumar 135 mm.*
197. A rare visitor to Academy Bay, this penguin was chasing small fish around the pier where my family keeps its boat. *Takumar 135 mm.*
198. Penguins are silhouetted against the morning sky before setting out on their daily feeding trips.
199. In the dull light after sunset these penguins remained still long enough for a slow exposure with the camera braced on a rock. *Takumar 135 mm.*
200. Excitement runs high as a hungry young hawk is intimidated by an even more frightened cormorant parent and its chick. After a few shy attempts, the raptor departed in order to beg for food from its parents. *Takumar 135 mm.*
201. Although most other young seabirds have white downy plumage, flightless cormorant chicks are a sooty black color. *Takumar 135 mm.*
202. The flightless cormorant is among those birds which are least afraid of people, and it readily allows itself to be approached up to a meter. *Takumar 135 mm.*
203. As the sun pierces the morning fog lying over the cool seas around Fernandina, a flightless cormorant stretches his ragged wings to dry. *Photo by André De Roy.*
204. Like scarlet blossoms, displaying male frigates dot the green salt bushes of Darwin Bay during the peak of courtship. In the foreground are a newly formed pair as well as the skeleton of one of last year's immatures. *Takumar 24 mm.*
205. Old enough to remain on the nest unprotected, a frigate chick sits hunched up waiting for its parents to return with food. *Takumar 135 mm.*
206. In the early morning a female frigate briefly exposes the egg she is incubating. *Takumar 135 mm.*
207. Tufts of throat feathers appear scattered on a displaying frigate's distended air pouch. *Takumar 135 mm.*
208. Resplendent with his fully inflated pouch and delicate, metallic-looking feathers, a male frigate sits with his newly acquired mate, recognizable by her white chest and pink eyering. *Takumar 135 mm.*
209. From a flimsy nest platform, a frigate chick overlooks Darwin Bay. *Takumar 35 mm.*
210. Although the male frigate can inflate and deflate his display pouch at will, he occasionally flies with a full-size balloon. This often throws him off balance and must seriously impair his vision. *Takumar 135 mm.*
211. While its mother shields it from the weather and predatory neighbors, this young frigate

chick flexes its tiny wings between bouts of dozing off. *Takumar 135 mm.*

212–214. As soon as the returning parent alights on his nest, the chick begins to beg for food by bobbing its head up and down and screaming. Within a few minutes the adult usually allows it to plunge its head down its throat for a meal of regurgitated fish. *Takumar 135 mm.*

215. Every ten to twenty minutes this male frigate returned with a new twig which he had plucked from low shrubs in midflight to present to his mate. She then arranged them in the nest while he set out for more. *Macro-Takumar 50 mm.*

216. Perhaps more than a year old already, and quite capable of flying, a juvenile great frigate bird still awaits periodic visits from his food-bearing parents. *Takumar 135 mm.*

217. An immature magnificent frigate bird is differentiated from immature great frigate birds by a larger size and a completely white head and chest. *Takumar 135 mm.*

218. Frigates like to soar along cliff edges where there are good updrafts. Sitting on the cliff overlooking the beach in Darwin Bay gave me this eye-level shot of a male with a shriveled display pouch, presumably searching for nesting material. *Vivitar 330 mm.*

219, 220. The speed involved in a wild chase by frigates to steal a booby's food is a tough challenge to the photographer. I have wasted more film in trying to obtain such sequences than on any other subject. *Vivitar 300 mm.*

221. With frantic screams and all the speed he can master, a masked booby tries to elude a pursuing frigate. *Vivitar 300 mm.*

222. The towering lava cliff of Volcan Ecuador looms above a pair of roosting masked boobies. *Takumar 35 mm.*

223–225. Oblivious to my presence, masked boobies go through an intense bout of pair-bonding rituals, presenting each other with nesting material, mild antagonism, and appeasing look-away posture. *Takumar 135 mm.*

226. Even though the sun is still low, an incubating masked booby is panting from the heat on a windless morning in the warm season. *Takumar 135 mm.*

227. A masked booby and chick in the bright morning sunlight. *Takumar 135 mm.*

228. It will be some time before the young booby chick acquires a protective cover of down. In the meantime he must be shielded from sun and predators. *Takumar 135 mm.*

229. Nesting within half a meter of the tourist trail, this female blue-footed booby on an uninhabited island certainly sees more people by the time she raises her young than I do in a year. *Takumar 135 mm.*

230, 233. While the afternoon sun highlights the contours of this breeding booby, the white, guano-covered rocks reflect enough light to give details in the shade. *Takumar 135 mm.*

231. Febrile activity pervades a colony of blue-footed boobies in full display and bathed in the afternoon sunlight. In the distance the large volcanoes of Isabela and Fernandina are visible. *Takumar 24 mm.*

232. Displaying intensely to a nearby female, a male booby lifts his feet in a slow, well-timed dance that fully exposes his bright-blue webs. *Takumar 135 mm.*

234. A pair of blue-footed boobies backlit and outlined against the blue-shaded cliff of Vicente Roca. *Takumar 135 mm.*

235. Hazy morning sunlight envelops this calm family scene at one nest of blue-footed boobies among several others. *Takumar 135 mm.*

236. A newly formed pair of red-footed boobies of which one is of the white form, representative of about five percent of the Tower Island population. *Takumar 135 mm.*

237. Preparing to run a gauntlet of marauding frigates, also in search of nesting material, a red-footed booby takes off to return to his nest with a selected twig. *Takumar 135 mm.*

238, 240. On a gray day, the gray-brown plumage of the red-footed booby blends with the dry vegetation, but its bill and feet stand out brilliantly. *Takumar 135 mm.*

239. Shredded cloud hiding the morning sun provides a good backdrop for these displaying boobies. *Takumar 135 mm.*

241. Precisely as I snapped the shutter, this immature pelican that had been sitting near the base of a cliff decided to fly off; I thought I had missed the shot until I saw the result. *Takumar 135 mm.*

242. A brown pelican, greeting his mate at their nest in their mangroves, waves his head from side to side with wings and pouch extended. *Macro-Takumar 50 mm.*

243. With hoarse squawks young pelicans squabble as parents prepare to feed them. *Takumar 135 mm.*

244. The rising sun shines briefly into this otherwise shaded nest where a young chick awaits the return of his parents. *Takumar 135 mm.*

245. Nesting in a dark, narrow crevice, this immobile bird was photographed by using a slow shutter speed and reflecting some light into the nest with my white camera box. *Takumar 135 mm.*

246. Hovering in the wind, a tropic bird inspects a potential nesting site along a cliff face. *Takumar 135 mm.*

247. I stretched as high as possible in a small skiff to take this picture of an exceptionally well exposed nest in a cliff at Devil's Crown Island. *Takumar 135 mm.*

248. As dusk approaches, swallow-tailed gulls leave the nesting colony for their nighttime feeding areas far out at sea. *Takumar 135 mm.*

249. Heavy swells may destroy the nests of swallow-tailed gulls along the lower part of cliffs. When this unusually large wave hit the shore, a swarm of gulls took to the air. *Takumar 35 mm.*

250. Swallow-tailed gulls doze on the nest during the day. *Takumar 135 mm.*

251. Nocturnal in habits, swallow-tailed gulls often display and mate at dusk before leaving to feed. *Takumar 135 mm.*

252. A pair of swallow-tailed gulls sit close together before establishing their nest. *Takumar 135 mm.*

253. Lying precariously on sharp lava, I was unable to look into the viewfinder properly, thus the gulls in the background were a good stroke of luck. *Takumar 135 mm.*

254. Found on almost all cliffs in the Galápagos Islands, the brown noddy is also widespread around the world. *Takumar 135 mm.*

255. An incubating waved albatross often rearranges his position, shuffling the huge egg about with his large webs, and sometimes moving it dozens of meters before it hatches. *Takumar 135 mm.*

256. Fishing pelicans can sometimes be seen followed by one or two brown noddies; when a pelican plunges on a school of small fish, the noddies quickly alight on his head or back to snatch stunned or escaping victims. *Takumar 135 mm.*

257. When high tide fills the small lagoon in back of the beach in Darwin Bay, many lava gulls usually swim and bathe in the crystal-clear water. *Takumar 135 mm.*

258. Overcast weather brings out the softness of the plumage of the waved albatross. *Takumar 135 mm.*

259. Albatrosses do not make nests; the chicks wander about daily in and out of the thickets for shade and are recognized by their parents. *Takumar 135 mm.*

260. Lava gulls' nests are rarely seen, but the presence of eggs or chicks is usually announced by frantic screams and dive-bombing by the parents. The same behavior is used to drive off sea lions that may threaten the nest on low ground, where it is typically located. *Macro-Takumar 50 mm.*

261. An opportunity to photograph this elusive petrel came while I was sitting in a skiff tied to the stern of a small tourist boat. The cook was washing dishes and tiny fragments of fried fish were floating on the surface. *Takumar 135 mm.*

262. Audubon's shearwaters feed in large flocks offshore, diving erratically to pursue small fish; they make unnerving targets to focus a long lens on from a moving boat. *Vivitar 300 mm.*

263–272. Before they leave the nesting colony in December or January and migrate out to sea, pairs of waved albatrosses engage in frantic bouts of courtship display aimed at cementing their lifelong bond in view of the four-month separation until the next nesting season. The well-structured rituals are performed in rapid succession, usually during late afternoon. *Takumar 135 mm.*

273. These feeding flamingos stand out at their best in the dull light of late afternoon. *Vivitar 300 mm.*

274. Standing by the edge of a salt pond, this young flamingo chick will need both time and much food from its parents to acquire the long, thin legs necessary for wading in deep water. *Takumar 135 mm.*

275. In the quiet lagoon of Punta Cormorant, flamingos spread their wings in courtship display. *Takumar 135 mm.*

276. An incubating great blue heron ruffles his feathers threateningly at my approach; rainy weather highlights his colors. This shot came out on the very first roll of film that I exposed after getting my first single-lens reflex camera ten years ago, and it remains my best of a nesting heron. *Takumar 83 mm.*

277. A visitor to the islands that is shyer than most other birds, a common egret fishes in a mangrove-fringed lagoon in the early morning. *Takumar 135 mm.*

278. On a dull, cloudy day, an immature yellow-crowned night heron has ventured out to the edge of the mangrove thickets where he normally spends his days. *Takumar 135 mm.*

279. Looking down from a boulder onto this slaking lava heron, I caught the early-morning sun shining brightly into his golden eye. *Takumar 135 mm.*

280. Fur seals are secretive and prefer rugged, rocky shorelines to raise their young. *Macro-Takumar 50 mm.*

281. While cruising along the cliff base of Darwin

Bay in a small skiff, I snapped these resting fur seals in a cool cave. *Takumar 135 mm.*

282. His instinct somehow misled, this bull fur seal showed much interest in a sea lion cow—and got a hefty rebuff. This shot shows clearly the difference in size, shape, color, and fur between the two species. *Takumar 135 mm.*

283. When the sun makes it uncomfortably warm for the fur seals to sleep on shore, they may float about lazily on the surface of the water, such as these in the grottoes of James Bay. A polarizing filter adds clarity to the water. *Takumar 135 mm.*

284. A thin layer of clouds partially filters the sun, causing both water and sea lions to glisten like oil. *Macro-Takumar 500 mm.*

285. In a playful gang, sea lion pups drag and toss a marine iguana as a toy, preventing it from reaching the shoreline. However, they do not hurt their victims in such games. *Takumar 135 mm. with polarizing filter.*

286. This aggressive territorial bull charged me repeatedly while I was photographing playful pups. *Takumar 135 mm.*

287. Sea lion pups are easy to photograph as they pose playfully, intrigued by anything unusual, including people. *Takumar 135 mm.*

288. Met by warning snarls, a newborn pup has difficulty locating its mother among a group of cows. *Takumar 135 mm.*

289. Sleeping deeply as sea lions do, this pup never became aware of my presence. *Takumar 135 mm.*

290. The sun glistening on their wet fur, a young territorial bull sea lion (right) and a cow greet in the shallows. *Takumar 135 mm.*

291. As wave after wave crashes into the blow hole at Punta Suarez, a sea lion enjoys the cooling spray. *Takumar 135 mm.*

292. In a rare violent encounter, these bulls lashed at each other furiously for about a half hour, staining the tide pool with blood. *Takumar 135 mm.*

293. After driving off his badly bleeding opponent, the winner of the battle returned, shaking with exhaustion, to defend his hard-won, bloody pond. *Takumar 24 mm.*

294. The only access to this hidden cove for both sea lions and waves is through a crevice that pierces an eroded tuff cone at the base of Volcan Ecuador. *Takumar 24 mm.*

1

1. Galápagos hawk and steaming fumaroles. Alcedo caldera, Isabela.
2. Steaming lava flow one week old. Fernandina lake.
3. A volcanic eruption. Cerro Azul, Isabela.
4, 5, 6. During a three-week period of activity, lava is fountaining 150 meters into the air and flowing ten kilometers downslope. Cerro Azul, Isabela.

5

4

6

7

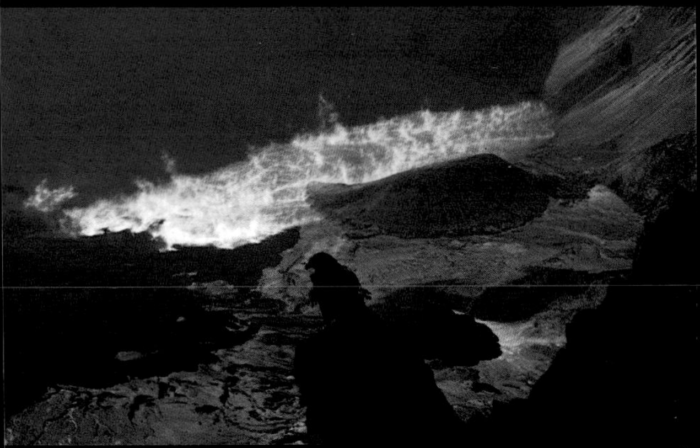

9

11

7, 8. Dormant caldera of Cerro Azul. Isabela.
9. Lake steaming two days after lava poured into it. Fernandina caldera.
10, 11. White-cheeked pintails on mineral lake. Fernandina caldera.

12

13

14

15

12, 18. Solitary volcano of Fernandina island.
13. Wildlife on the shoreline of Fernandina island.
14. Sulphur crystals inside fumarole vent. Alcedo, Isabela.
15. Sulphur fumaroles at Volcan de Azufre. Sierra Negra, Isabela.
16. Steam vent. Volcan Alcedo, Isabela.
17. Galápagos doves seeking moisture in fumarole. Fernandina.

16

17

18

19

20

22

23

24

19. Folds and flow patterns in pahoehoe lava. Sullivan Bay, Santiago.
20. Lava flows cutting through vegetation. Volcan Wolf, Isabela.
21. Steaming fumaroles and dew-laden spider web. Sierra Negra, Isabela.
22. Solidified cascades of lava. Caldera of Cerro Azul, Isabela.
23. Cracked lava surface. Sullivan Bay, Santiago.
24. Tuff cones and crater. James Bay, Santiago.

21

25

26

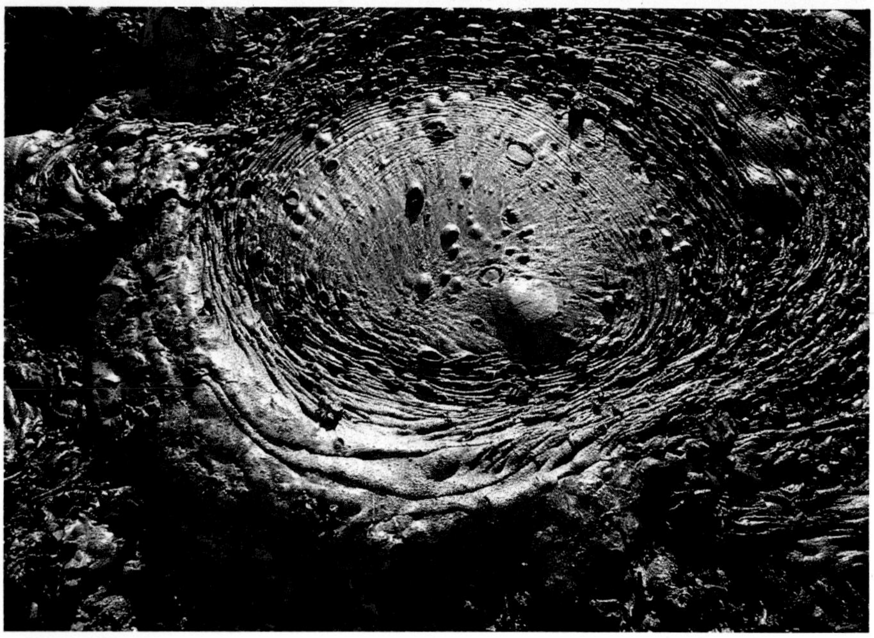

27

28

25–28. Details of eighty-year-old pahoehoe lava flow. Sullivan Bay, Santiago.

29. Overlapping lava flows. Slope of Volcan Wolf, Isabela.
30. A *Mollugo* plant, early colonizer of new volcanic terrain. Sullivan Bay, Santiago.
31. Scoria and spatter cones. Sierra Negra, Isabela.

29

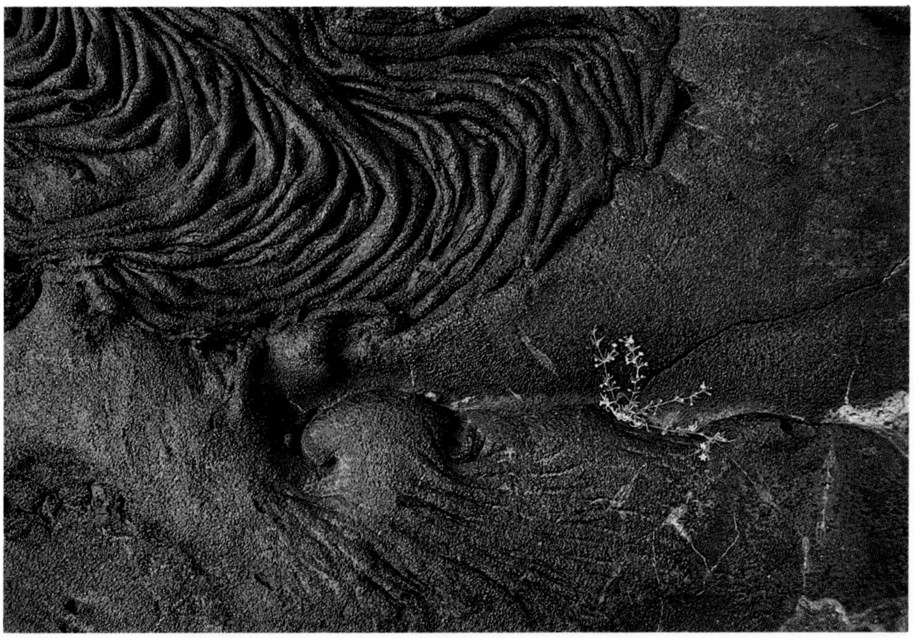

30

31

32

33

34

35

32. Pahoehoe lava which has covered older terrain. Sullivan Bay, Santiago.

33. *Brachycereus* cactus, pioneer of fresh lava flows. Sullivan Bay, Santiago.

34. Lava molds of *Brachycereus* cactus. Tower.

35. Frozen lava rivers and *Brachycereus* cactus. Sullivan Bay, Santiago.

38

36. Early morning blossom of *Brachycereus* cactus. Punta Espinosa, Fernandina.
37. Large coral heads stranded by uplift of Urvina Bay in 1954. Isabela.
38. Arid vegetation on lava terrain. Academy Bay, Santa Cruz.

36

37

39. *Opuntia* cactus. Pinzon.
40, 41, 43. Flowers of three different varieties of *Opuntia* cactus—respectively, Champion Island, Isabela, and Plazas.

39

40

41

42

43

44

42. *Jasminocereus* cactus blossom. Isabela.
44. Forest of *Opuntia* cactus. Barrington.

ARID ZONE VEGETATION

45. *Scalesia incisa.* Pinzon.
46, 56. *Scalesia villosa.* Floreana.
47. *Bursera.* Tagus Cove, Isabela.
48. *Sesuvium.* South Plaza.
49. *Tiquilia* (*Coldenia*). Bartolomé.
50. *Polygala.* Floreana.
51. *Bursera* and *Erythrina.* Salt mine, Santiago.

45

46

47

48

49

50

52

53

52. *Cordia.* Santa Cruz.
53, 58. *Portulaca.* South Plaza.
54. Wild Tomato *Lycopersicon.* Fernandina.
55. *Erythrina.* Santa Cruz.
57. *Ipomoea.* Fernandina.

55

54 56

57

58

HIGHLAND VEGETATION

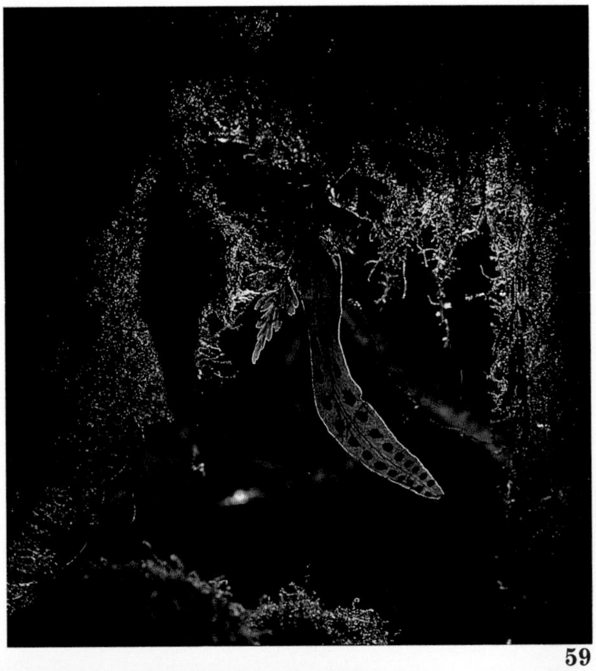

59

60

61

66

62

63

64

59. *Polypodium* fern. Alcedo, Isabela.
60. *Elaterium*. Santa Cruz.
61. *Scalesia pedunculata*. Santa Cruz.
62. *Lycopodium*. Santa Cruz.
63. *Ludwigia*. Santa Cruz.
64. Bromeliad, *Tillandsia*. Floreana.
65. *Tournefortia*. Santa Cruz.
66. *Scalesia* forest, summit of Santa Cruz.

65

67

68

70

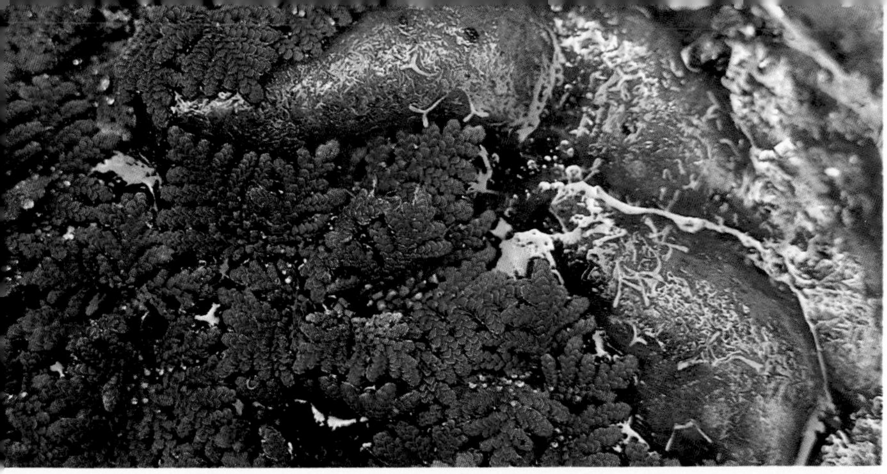

69

HIGHLAND VEGETATION

67. Tree fern, *Cyathea.* Santa Cruz.
68. *Ipomoea* alba. Alcedo, Isabela.
69. Floating fern, *Azolla.* Santa Cruz.
70. *Miconia robinsoniana.* Santa Cruz.

71, 80. Male vermilion flycatchers. Santa Cruz.
72. Sphinx moth. Alcedo, Isabela.
73. Spider eating cockroach. Santa Cruz.
74. Spider among cactus spines. Santa Cruz.
75. Spider and web. Alcedo, Isabela.

71

72

73

74

75

76

76. *Bulimulus* land snail on fern spores. Alcedo, Isabela.
77. Grasshopper eating *Scalesia*. Floreana.
78. Yellow warblers. Santa Cruz.
79. Large-billed flycatcher. Santa Cruz.
81. Female vermilion flycatcher. Santa Cruz.
82. Diurnal moth. Alcedo, Isabela.

77

78

79

80

81

82

83

84

86

85

83. Short-eared owl. Santa Cruz.
84, 85. Galápagos rails. Santa Cruz.
86. Mangrove lagoon. Elizabeth Bay, Isabela.

87

88

89

87. Rays. Turtle Cove, Santa Cruz.
88. Green sea turtle. Elizabeth Bay, Isabela.
89. Seascape. Punta Espinosa, Fernandina.
90. Blow hole. Punta Suarez, Hood.
91. Bottlenose dolphin.

90

91

94

92

93

92. Buccaneer Cove, Santiago.
93. Cape Douglas, Fernandina.
94. Sea lions. Sullivan Bay, Santiago.

95

9

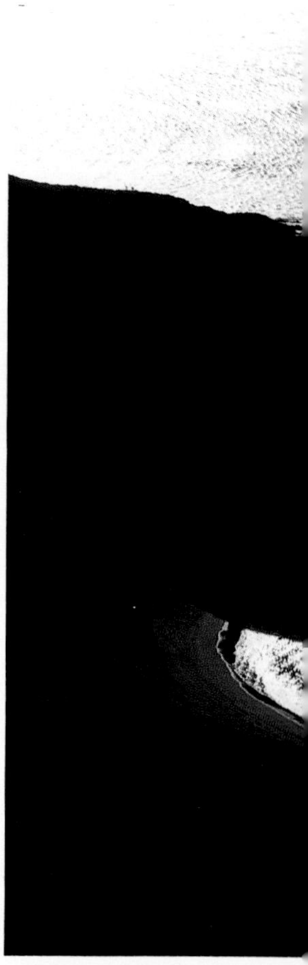

97

95. Punta Espinosa, Fernandina.
96. Bainbridge Rock.
97. Devil's Crown, Floreana.
98. Buccaneer Cove, Santiago.

98

99

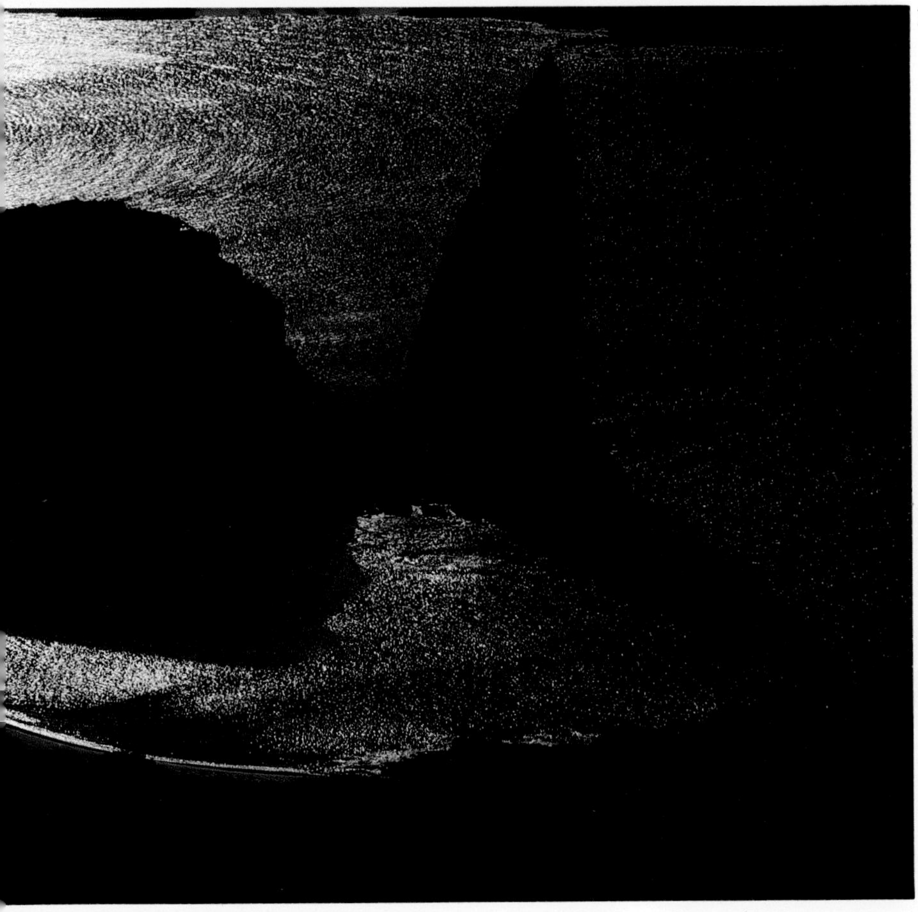
100

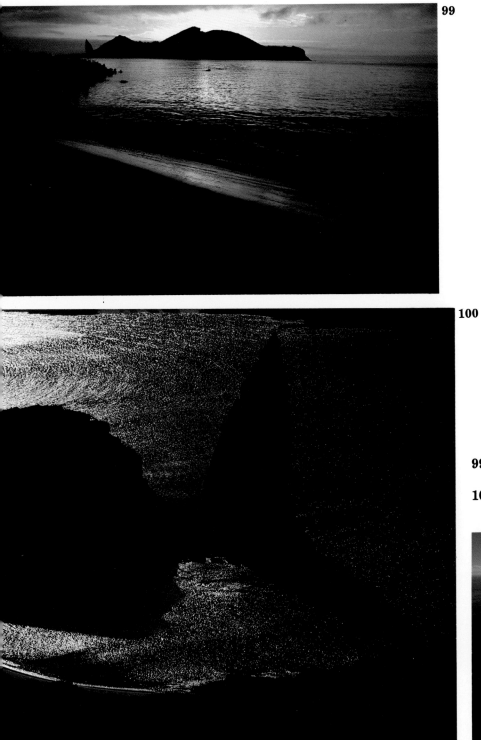

99–103. Bartolomé Island, near Santiago.
104. Marine iguanas and morning fog. Cape Douglas, Fernandina.

101

102

103

105

106

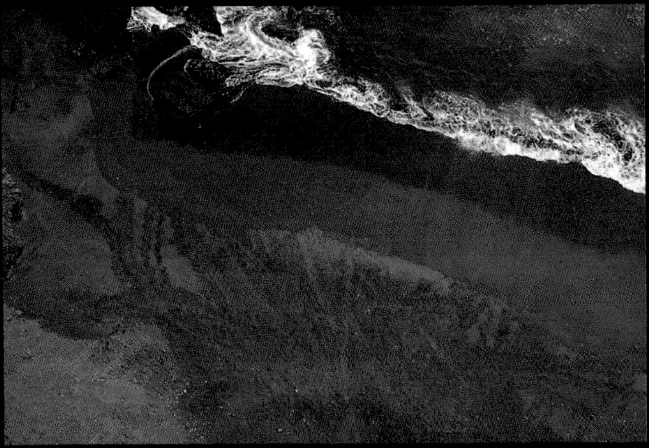
107

108

109

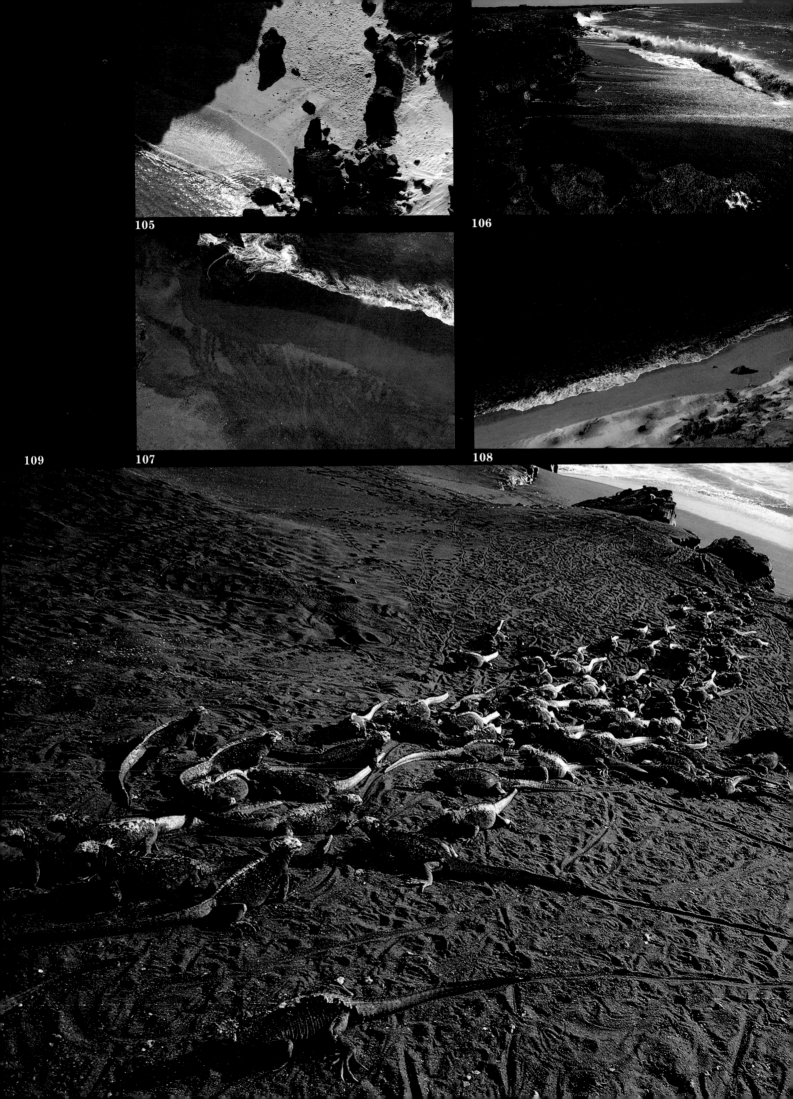

110

111

112 113

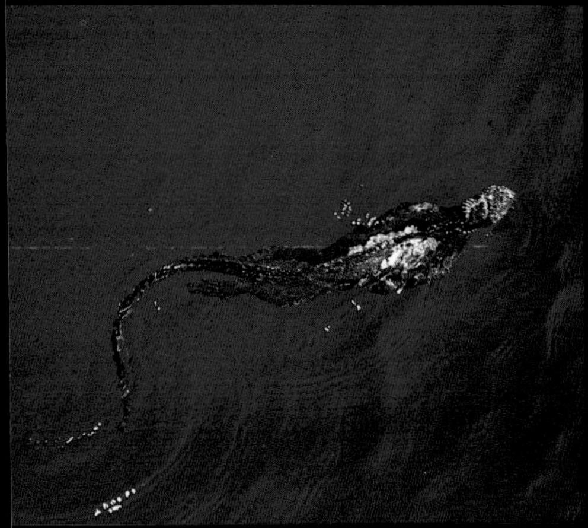

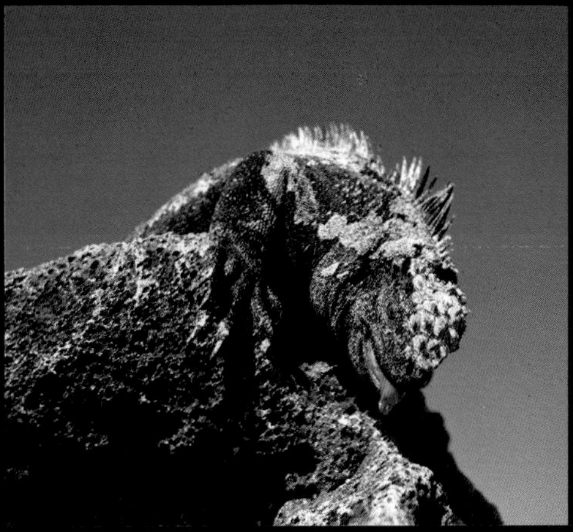

114 115

105. Sea lion tracks, Bainbridge Rock.
106. Lava sand. Cape Douglas, Fernandina.
107. Sea lion tracks. Buccaneer Cove, Santiago.
108. Turtle nests. Bartolomé.
109, 115. Marine iguanas. Cape Douglas, Fernandina.
110. Marine iguana. Santa Cruz.
111. Feeding marine iguanas. Santiago.
112, 113. Basking marine iguanas. Punta Espinosa, Fernandina.
114. Swimming marine iguana. Santiago.

117

116

118

119

116. Nesting female marine iguanas. Punta Espinosa, Fernandina.
117. Marine iguana feeding in tide pool. Hood.
118. Male marine iguana. Hood.
119. Marine iguana and sally light-foot crabs. Hood.
120. Territorial male marine iguana with females. Punta Suarez, Hood.
121, 122. Lava lizard on marine iguana. Fernandina.

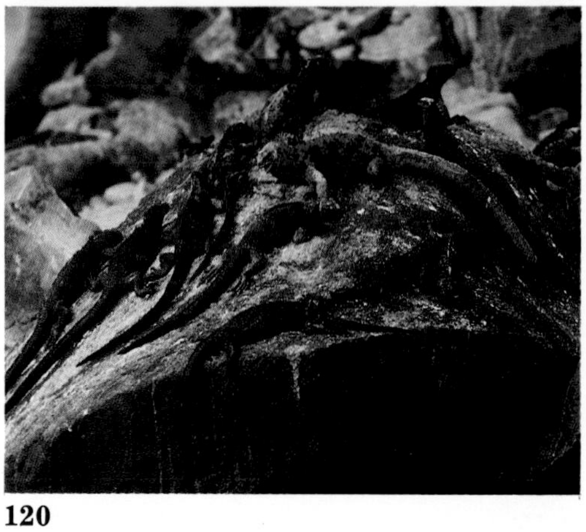

120

121

123. Male marine iguana. Punta Albemarle, Isabela.
124. Marine iguana in blow-hole spray. Punta Suavez, Hood.

122

123

125

126

127

128

25. Cannibalism in lava lizards. Plazas.
26. Female lava lizard. Hood.
27. Lava lizard eating grasshopper. Seymour.
28. Male lava lizard. Santiago.

130

129. Lava lizard and Darwin's finch seeking flies and ticks. Punta Espinosa, Fernandina.
130. Female lava lizard. Santiago.
131. Male lava lizards fighting. Santa Cruz.

132 133

134

135

132. Lava lizard. Santa Cruz.
133, 135. Lava lizard being eaten by Galápagos snake. Santiago.
134. Galápagos snake. Fernandina.

136

137

13

140

141

136. Male land iguana. Beagle crater, Isabela.
137. Hatchling land iguana. Fernandina.
138. Male land iguana. Conway Bay, Santa Cruz.
139. Land iguana. Fernandina caldera.
140. Male land iguana. Fernandina.
141. Basking group of land iguanas. Caldera rim, Fernandina.

144

145

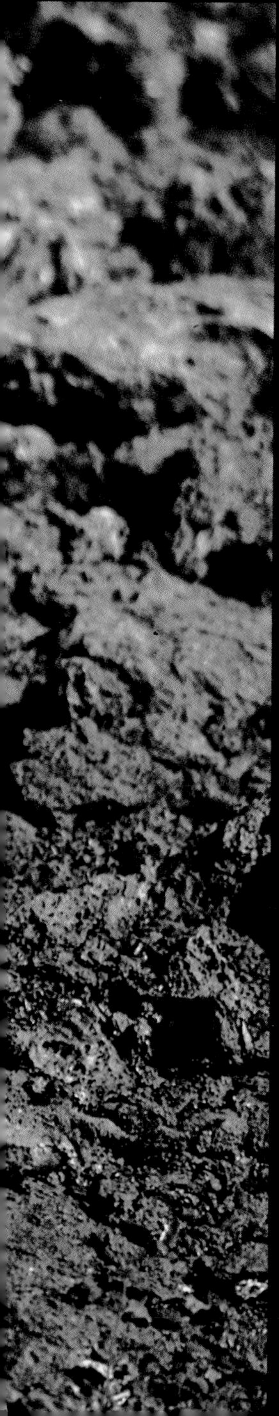

146

147

142. Land iguana eating *Portulaca* blossom. Plaza.
143. Fighting male land iguanas. Fernandina.
144. Mocking bird picking dry skin from land iguana. Fernandina.
145. Land iguana eating cactus pad. Fernandina.
146. Land iguana. Caldera rim, Fernandina.
147. Male land iguana. Barrington.

149

150

151

148. Giant tortoises amid steaming fumaroles. Alcedo, Isabela.
149. Darwin's finch ridding responsive tortoise of ticks. Alcedo, Isabela.
150. Galápagos hawk and giant tortoises at sunrise. Alcedo, Isabela.
151. Tortoise in mud wallow. Alcedo, Isabela.
152. Tortoises in rain pond. Alcedo, Isabela.
153. Large tortoise grazing. Alcedo, Isabela.
154. First rain of the season. Alcedo, Isabela.
155. Concentration of tortoises in temporary rain pond. Alcedo,

153

154

155

156

157

158

159

160

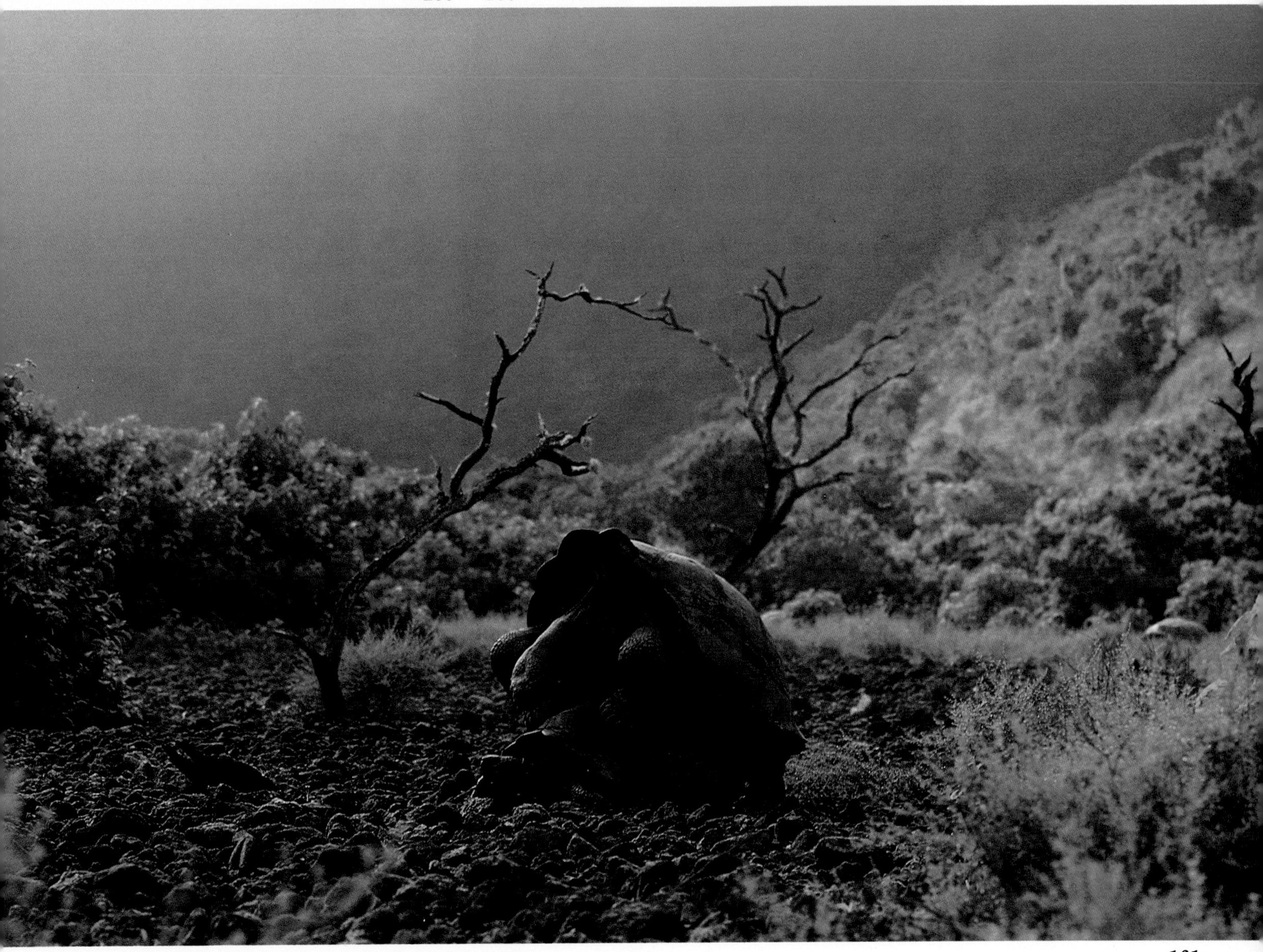
161

156. Tortoise aggressive display in fumarole area. Alcedo, Isabela.
157. Sun-bleached tortoise skeleton. Alcedo, Isabela.
158. Foggy morning in rainy season. Alcedo, Isabela.
159, 161. Mating tortoises. Alcedo, Isabela.
160. Hatchling tortoises emerging from nest. Alcedo, Isabela.

163

162

162. Saddleback tortoise. Pinzon.
163. Pinta Island tortoise. Darwin Station.
164. Hood Island tortoise. Darwin Station.

164

165

167

165. Saddleback tortoise eating cactus pad. Pinzon.
166, 167. Browsing saddleback tortoise. Pinzon.

166

168

169

170

168. Small ground finch, most common of the thirteen species. Alcedo, Isabela.
169. Small ground finch in typical side-entrance nest. Santa Cruz.
170. Medium ground finch feeding on *Erythrina* blossoms. Santa Cruz.
171. Agile foraging behavior of small tree finch. Santa Cruz.

171

173

174

175

176

177

178

179

180

183

181

182

172. Large ground finch—*Geospiza magnirostris.*
173. Small ground finch—*Geospiza fuliginosa.*
174. Sharp-beaked ground finch—*Geospiza difficilis.*
175. Cactus finch—*Geospiza scandeus.*
176. Large cactus finch—*Geospiza conirostris.*
177. Vegetarian finch—*Platyspiza crassirostris.*
178. Small tree finch—*Camarhynchus parvulus.*
179. Large tree finch—*Camarhynchus psittacula.*
180. Woodpecker finch—*Camarhynchus pallidus.*
181. Mangrove finch—*Camarhynchus heliobates.*
182. Medium ground finch—*Geospiza fortis.*
183. Warbler finch—*Certhidea olivacea.*

184

184. Floreana mockingbird. Champion.
185. Hood mockingbird. Punta Suarez.
186. Galápagos dove nesting in abandoned iguana burrow. Fernandina.
187. Galápagos mockingbird. Fernandina.
188. Galápagos dove. Pinzon.

185

186

187

188

189

193

GALÁPAGOS HAWKS

189. Inside Fernandina caldera.
190–192. Alcedo.
193. Nest. Santiago.
194. Alcedo caldera.
195. Fernandina caldera.
196. Adult preying on marine iguana. Fernandina.

190

191

192

194

195

196

197

198

199

197. Penguin under water. Academy Bay, Santa Cruz.

198. Galápagos penguins. Punta Espinosa, Fernandina.

199. Galápagos penguins at dusk. Punta Espinosa, Fernandina.

200. Confrontation between immature hawk and flightless cormorant parent and chick. Cape Douglas, Fernandina.

201. Flightless cormorant feeding young. Punta Espinosa, Fernandina.

202. Flightless cormorant. Punta Espinosa, Fernandina.

203. Flightless cormorant drying wings. Cape Douglas, Fernandina.

200

202

201

GREAT FRIGATE BIRDS

205

206

207

208

204. Nesting colony in display season. Tower.
205. Four-month-old chick. Tower.
206. Female incubating. Tower.
207, 210. Male with inflated display pouch. Tower.
208. Newly mated pair. Tower.

209

210 211

212

215

216. Immature great frigate bird. Tower.
217. Immature magnificent frigate bird. Seymour.
218. Male great frigate bird with shrunken display pouch. Tower.
219, 220. Harassing great frigates grab a red-footed booby by the tail, then catch the fish it has dropped. Tower.
221. Pirating great frigate pursuing masked booby. Tower.

216

217

219

220

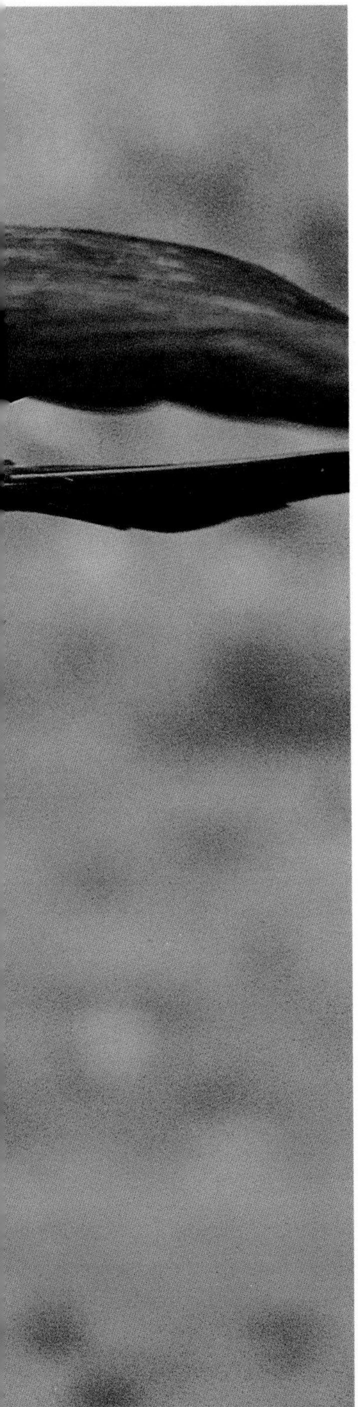

218

221

223

224

225

226

227

228

MASKED BOOBIES

222. A pair at Punta Vicente Roca, Isabela.
223-225. Courtship and nest building. Tower.
226. Incubating with webbed feet wrapped around egg. Daphne.
227. Chick with parent. Tower.
228. Parent shading naked hatchling. Daphne.

229

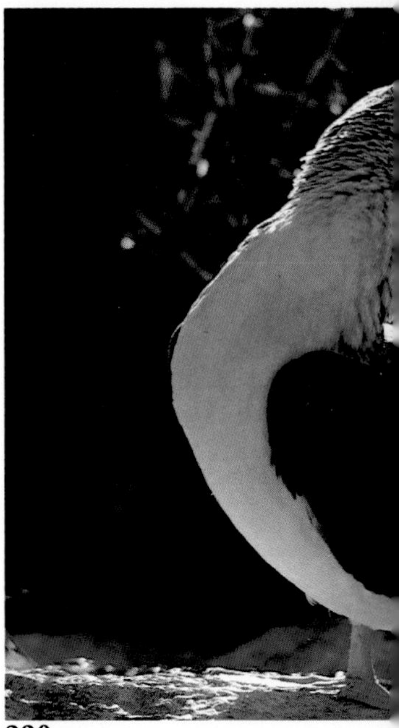

230

231

232

233

234

BLUE-FOOTED BOOBIES

229. Female incubating. Hood.
230, 233. Preening. Hood.
231. Colony in courtship display. Fernandina.
232. Courtship dance. Hood.
234. Pair, female (left) largest. Isabela.
235. Blue-footed booby pair, with chick; note large pupil of female. Isabela.

236

237

238

239

240

RED-FOOTED BOOBIES

236. Mixed pair showing both color phases. Tower.
237. Gathering nesting material. Tower.
238. Male skypointing display. Tower.
239. Courting pair. Tower.
240. Perched in *Cordia* bush. Tower.

241

242

243

244

241. Immature brown pelican. Academy Bay, Santa Cruz.
242, 243. Brown pelicans. Academy Bay, Santa Cruz.
244. Tropic bird chick. Daphne.
245, 247. Red-billed tropic birds nesting in cliff cavities. Devil's Crown.
246. Red-billed tropic bird in flight.

245

246

SWALLOW TAIL GULLS

248

248. In flight. Plazas.
249. Punta Suarez. Hood.
250. Incubating. Tower.
251. Mating at sunset. Tower
252. Pair. Plazas.
253. With chick. Tower.

249

250

251

252

253

254

255

256

254. Brown noddy. Academy Bay, Santa Cruz.
255, 258. Waved albatross. Hood.
256. Brown noddy fishing with brown pelican. Academy Bay, Santa Cruz.
257. Lava gull. Tower.
259. Waved albatross chick. Hood.
260. Lava gull nest. Mosovera.

257

258

259

260

261

261. White-vented storm petrel. Punta Espinosa, Fernandina.
262. Audubon's shearwater. Academy Bay, Santa Cruz.
263-272. Courtship display of waved albatross. Hood.
273. Flamingos feeding. Punta Cormorant, Floreana. ◦
274. Flamingo chick. Salt mine, Santiago.
275. Courtship display of greater flamingos. Punta Cormorant, Floreana.

263

264

265

266

267

268

269

270

271

272

273

274

277

278

279

276. Great blue heron. Academy Bay, Santa Cruz.
277. Common egret. Academy Bay, Santa Cruz.
278. Immature yellow-crowned night heron. Santa Cruz.

280

281

282

283

279. Lava heron. Punta Espinosa, Fernandina.

280. Fur seal mother nursing pup. Cape Douglas, Fernandina.

281. Fur seal bull and females. Tower.

282. Fur seal bull confronting sea lion cow. Cape Douglas, Fernandina.

283. Fur seals. James Bay.

284

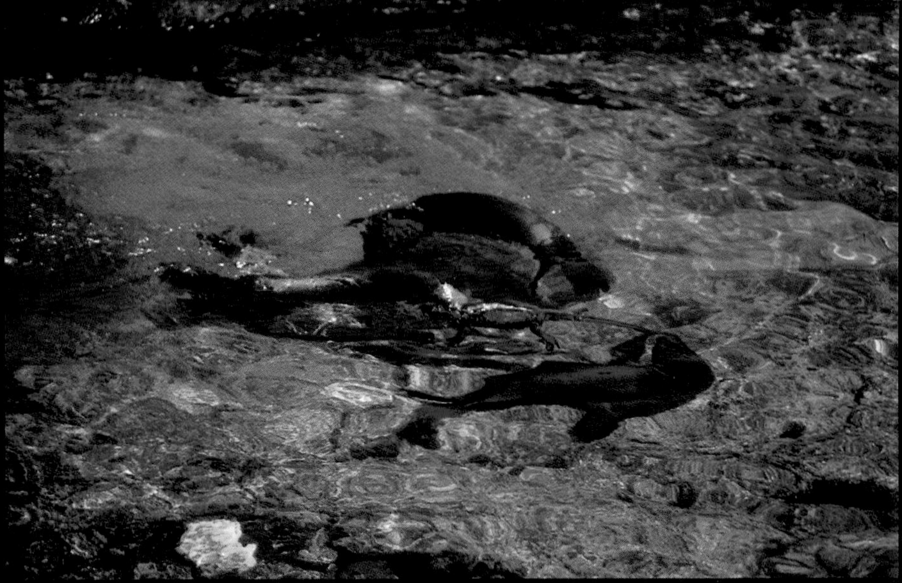

285

286

287

284. Congenial sleeping cow sea lions. Punta Suarez, Hood.
285. Playful young sea lions dragging marine iguana. Punta Espinosa, Fernandina.
286. Territorial sea lion bull with young. Seymour.
287. Sea lion pup. Punta Suarez, Hood.
288. Sea lion cows with newborn pup. Punta Espinosa, Fernandina.
289. Sleeping sea lion pup. Punta Espinosa, Fernandina.
290. Sea lion bull and cow. Punta Espinosa, Fernandina.
291. Sea lion at blow hole. Punta Suarez, Hood.
292. Territorial fight between lion bulls. Cape Douglas, Fernandina.
293. The victor in blood-stained tidepool after driving off opponent. Cape Douglas, Fernandina.
294. Small sea lion colony in sheltered cove. Punta Vicente Roca, Isabela.

288

289

290

291

292

293